Pitt Press Series

SELECTIONS

FROM

VIRGIL'S GEORGICS

SELECTIONS

FROM

VIRGIL'S GEORGICS

EDITED BY

JOHN MASSON, M.A., LL.D.

CAMBRIDGE
AT THE UNIVERSITY PRESS
1921

CAMBRIDGE
UNIVERSITY PRESS

University Printing House, Cambridge CB2 8BS, United Kingdom

Cambridge University Press is part of the University of Cambridge.

It furthers the University's mission by disseminating knowledge in the pursuit of
education, learning and research at the highest international levels of excellence.

www.cambridge.org
Information on this title: www.cambridge.org/9781107487161

© Cambridge University Press 1921

First published 1921
First paperback edition 2015

A catalogue record for this publication is available from the British Library

ISBN 978-1-107-48716-1 Paperback

PREFACE

THAT excellent scholar, Mr T. E. Page, says in the preface to his edition of the *Georgics*, "Young students seem now to limit their reading of Virgil chiefly to the *Aeneid*." Mr Hirzel again, the editor of Virgil in the Oxford Classical Texts, writes in the *Classical Review* of "the unmerited oblivion into which the *Bucolics* and *Georgics* have fallen at our public schools." I find, on pretty wide enquiry, that as a rule very few pupils read more than a single *Georgic* before leaving school.

There exists a quite proper prejudice against reading mere extracts from any great poem. But to select from the *Georgics* is quite a different thing from selecting parts out of *Aeneid* I or II or VI. In each of the latter to omit a single scene is to cut off an organic part of the book. The *Georgics* is largely a descriptive and meditative poem which embodies much technical matter and young readers soon weary of description, even when done by a master-hand. It is not surprising that teachers of Classics should prefer the *Aeneid*, which possesses the interest of narrative and incident which the *Georgics* lack. But to make up for these drawbacks there are, scattered over the four books, many different passages of wide range and deep human interest. In these much of Virgil's best known and most characteristic writing is to be found. They show his practical 'philosophy' and attitude to life and reveal how profoundly his country's tragedy, in an age of Revolution like our own, had shaken and remoulded all his outlook. The personality and ideals of the poet come out so clearly in these passages that they help us to understand the *Aeneid* better in its meaning both for Virgil's own age and for all time.

The present edition is meant to meet the needs of pupils in the higher classes of Secondary Schools and those of the 'ordinary' Latin Class in the Scottish Universities. Lovers of Virgil may also find it convenient to have these passages collected.

The Introduction is intended to appeal both to younger and older students of Virgil's works in general and will, it is hoped, add to the interest of the book. Thanks mainly to British scholars we can now estimate the poem far better as reflecting the history of the time. Moreover recent research has thrown fresh light on all Virgil's earlier writings especially in relation to the poets of his day[1]. I have tried to point out the relation of the *Georgics* both to his earlier and to his later work and thus to show Virgil's steady growth both in thought and art.

The influence of Lucretius is also discussed both in the earlier admiration for Epicurean science, which Virgil soon outgrew, and also in the deeper and lifelong enthusiasm which helped in great part to make him, more than all others, 'the Humanist Poet.'

British scholars from Conington, first and foremost, down to Page and Sidgwick have done such admirable work on the *Georgics* that not much room is left for fresh interpretation of the poem. A more conscientious editor than Conington could not be found: he passes over no difficulty, and is careful to admit to the full the force of any evidence for an interpretation even when he himself rejects it. It must be admitted that Virgil's language is frequently

---

[1] These results are skilfully summed up by Mr Mackail in an admirable paper, "Virgil and Virgilianism" (*Classical Review* for 1908).

obscure so that we cannot decide which of several possible meanings he intended.

Sunt lacrimae rerum et mentem mortalia tangunt.

Who can tell the exact meaning of this line? (Perhaps its strength may be partly in the very vagueness, which widens its application.) Munro regrets that Virgil lacks "the transparent clearness of Ovid." Water may be clear because it is shallow. It must be admitted that Virgil at times "shadows out more meanings than one, not discriminating them in his own mind as sharply as they must be distinguished by a modern commentator[1]." The *Georgics* offer fewer difficulties than the *Aeneid* with its frequent inversions and transferences of construction[2] and, not least, by "his habit of hinting at two or three modes of expression, while actually employing one[3]." But Virgil is in general difficult to translate. The position of a word, the choice of one synonym rather than another, may affect the meaning of a sentence in his case far more than in other writers. No commentator on the poet has equalled Conington in instinctive perception of such points: sometimes he may, with intention, overstress their force, but always with marvellous intuition of the relation of single words or phrases to the whole sentence. In the notes his readings have been frequently quoted and emphasized as a valuable lesson for the young student in the fine art of translating[4]. They make him realize the diffi-

---

[1] For a simple instance see Conington's note on *G.* III, 9, and *Aen.* II, I.

[2] See note on *G.* IV, 50 in the present volume.

[3] Conington, Preface to verse-translation, 1879, p. xiv.

[4] See for instance the lines

> Quo fletu manes, qua numina voce moveret?
> Illa quidem Stygia nabat iam frigida cumba.
>
> *G.* IV, 505–6.

Conington's rendering may be over-stressed but he has caught

culties of 'conscientious rendering,' and often the almost impossibility of reconciling exact scholarship and the exacting literary sense which asks not merely an equivalent for each clause but demands also the spirit which binds all clauses together in a living, glowing sentence.

I am much indebted to Mr Page's commentary, which is extremely thorough and helpful. Sidgwick's brief notes are very much to the point and his Index of style is valuable as referring Virgil's peculiarities to general principles. Keightley's edition is very serviceable from his knowledge of ancient and modern husbandry in Italy as well as at home. For all that appeals to the naturalist, especially in *Georgic* IV, Mr Royds' interesting book, *Beasts, Birds and Bees of Virgil* (second edition, 1918), has been helpful.

Conington says, "There are few writers whose text is in so satisfactory a state as Virgil's." This is due to the fact that of our best MSS. several date from the fourth century. Moreover the text was from the first century the subject of close study by grammarians and commentators, much of whose work is preserved. A few important variants are discussed in their place.

Amongst many writers on Virgil, British and foreign, I am specially indebted to Sellar, whose admirable work is so condensed that it will always be read more by the scholar than by the young student, also to Sainte-Beuve's delightful *Étude sur Virgile.* Édouard Goumy's *Les Latins* (1892) is also useful. Dr T. R. Glover's very readable book treats ably the influences, literary and national, which moulded the poet's outlook. Dr Warde Fowler's *Social Life at*

the spirit of both lines and the relation of one to the other. Compare again at *Aen.* IV, 382 his version of "si quid pia numina possunt," or, at so different a passage as *G.* I, 79–81 his rendering of the effect given by the position of *arida tantum* and *effetos.*

Rome in the age of Cicero throws a flood of light on the
historical background of Virgil's poem. The book
makes the period of Virgil's earlier manhood with all
its human problems live before us, like some familiar
landscape seen from a fresh height. It is to be
regretted that the same scholar did not perform for
the *Georgics* what he has done for the last half of the
Aeneid, in his treatment of which 'science' in the shape
of profound scholarship works hand in hand with
intuition to most fruitful result. I am indebted to
Dr Fowler for revising my list of Selections and
suggesting several changes which have been carried
out.

I have gained much from discussing a number of
the passages with a scholar of so wide a range as
Professor Grierson. I also owe valuable suggestions
to my friend, Mr H. A. Webster, late Librarian to
the University of Edinburgh.

Professor Grierson allows me to quote the following
from a letter of his which expresses the growing sense
of the importance of making the best work of those
Latin authors, by whom English writers have been
most influenced, easily accessible to the real student
of English Literature. It is hoped that these selections
may be of some service in this way.

"I read your Introduction to your *Selections from
Virgil's Georgics* with the greatest interest. It is just
such a book as I should like to be able to ask my
English Honours Students to read and study. I am
always being made to feel the need of some more
extended and literary study of Classical Literature
than most of them bring with them from school. But
time is limited and there must be some selection.
I believe that both teachers and publishers will have
to consider the necessity for focussing classical reading
on our own Literature—I mean selecting what is read

CONTENTS

INTRODUCTION

I. HISTORICAL

Virgil's life falls during prolonged Civil Wars. Relation of his countrymen North of the Po to Julius Caesar and to Augustus. Gain of the entire Roman world from the Empire. Virgil's personal debt to Augustus.

MOST of Virgil's life fell amid the confusion and distress of civil strife. He was born on the 15th of October, 70 B.C., at Andes, a hamlet near Mantua in Cisalpine Gaul. This means that he was not a Roman, but one of those Italians who had suffered under the injustice and oppression of the Senate, which styled itself 'the Republic' but was in reality an Oligarchy of very extreme type. The Italians had paid taxes and fought in Rome's armies; they were in every way equal to Roman citizens but Rome had persistently refused them the rights of citizenship until, 20 years before the birth of Virgil, they had extorted them, in part at least, through the Social War. Even after this Rome schemed to make the new privileges of no effect. The weakness of the Senate's rule had been shown in a long series of Civil Wars. From 145–80 B.C. those had raged over Italy like a tempest, deadly and terrific, passing away but only to return again until the death of Sulla in 78 B.C. In two years of the Social War alone, from 90 to 89, 300,000 men were said to have been slain. Again and again Italy had known times like that in French history which is called 'La Terreur.' Cicero says, "The horror of those times is so burned into our country that it seems as if not merely men but even brute creatures could not endure the thought of their returning[1]." In the provinces oppression and misrule had become intolerable. For one Verres brought to justice by Cicero's splendid patriotism

[1] *Catiline Orations*, II, c. 9.

and talent countless governors returned to Rome with fortunes wrung from their wretched subjects. In Italy itself the vast number of slaves was a cause both of anxiety and of national degradation. In 73 the Slave War and in 63 the Conspiracy of Catiline showed in alarming forms the general discontent and the undermined foundations of the State. The country was ripe for revolution but leaders such as Catiline who professed to aim at redressing injustice could only have substituted a still grosser tyranny. In 49 Caesar crossed the Rubicon and civil war began afresh.

But the rise of Julius Caesar had brought new hope to the world. In him men saw a leader of real genius, a man absolutely fearless, deeply sensitive to the incompetence of the Government and the gross injustice done to the poorer citizens and to the Provincials. After many attempts to win reform from the Senate, he recognised that the task was hopeless. As he said, "The Republic is nothing—a mere name without substance or form." For this he was determined to substitute a Government that was real. As Consul he had carried over the heads of the Senate those 'Julian Laws' which were welcomed by all honest men as checking the gross abuses and meeting the needs of the time. He was specially interested in securing justice for the Provincials. In 49 B.C., when Virgil was in his 21st year, the Transpadani too received the full rights of citizenship which Caesar had long striven to secure for them. Northern Italians like Virgil must have watched his glorious career at home and abroad with gratitude and love as well as admiration. To them he was both hero and liberator. Hirtius, who continues Caesar's record of the Gallic War, tells us that Caesar, then Governor of Cisalpine Gaul, visited his province early in 50 B.C. and was received in the district north of the Po—Virgil's own country—"with incredible marks of honour and affection. Nothing that could be devised for the decoration of the roads, the gates and all places which he was going to pass through, was left undone. The whole populace along with their children went forth to meet him[1]." We can well understand the horror expressed by Virgil and felt by all his countrymen at Caesar's murder and also the gratitude which was transferred to his adopted heir.

Octavian (soon to be known as Augustus) strove so far as in him lay to carry out Caesar's aims, possibly with more success in the field of home politics than Julius himself could have done, since he did not attempt more than average men were likely to tolerate. A great part of his adopted father's prestige fell on himself. Under him Italy was to enjoy peace and prosperity long unknown to it. To the general gratitude for the many benefits of his rule there was added in Virgil's case a deep personal debt. In the Civil War Cremona had sympathised with the Senatorial party. After the battle of Philippi in B.C. 42, Octavian and Antony, who had to reward their victorious soldiers with land, confiscated for the purpose the country about Cremona and the neighbouring Mantua including Virgil's farm. The poet's life was endangered at the hands of the soldier who took possession of his land. He then journeyed to Rome and was reinstated in his property by Augustus at the intercession of his friends Pollio, Gallus and Varius, the former two being soldiers and men of action as well as writers. The event is recorded under slight disguise in the first *Eclogue*, in the form of a dialogue between Tityrus the poet and his fellow-shepherd Meliboeus. The latter is one of many who have been evicted and left to seek a home in some foreign land. "It is a God," says Tityrus, "who has created for me the peace you see: for a God he will ever be to me. He it is who has made my kine free to wander at large and myself to play at my pleasure on my shepherd's pipe." Thus threatened with poverty which would rob him of the leisure to study and write, Virgil never forgot that he owed to Octavian the restoration of his broken career.

A French scholar writes, "The *Georgics* had the great honour of being the first greeting, the first homage, the

[1] *De Bello Gallico*, viii, 51.

first cry of gratitude addressed by a poet in the name of the entire Roman world to a man in whom was incarnated that Revolution to which the world was destined to owe the two great centuries of 'Roman Peace,' *Pax Romana*[1]." Except for the Oligarchy whose unjust privileges had been cut away, and a few extremists like Brutus with whom the name of 'Republic' counted for more than the reality, this statement holds good. There was a feeling in the air that the world was entering upon a new era, free from the terrors and oppression of the past, and so it proved to be. The Alexandrian Jew, Philo, writing about A.D. 41, says of Augustus that, when he entered upon rule, Civil War was raging over the whole world and "the whole race of mankind would very nearly have been destroyed by mutual slaughter but for his control. He gave freedom to every city, he civilised nations which before were savage, he was the guardian of peace; he distributed to every man his due portion, he offered favours to all ungrudgingly, he never in his whole life concealed or reserved for himself anything that was good or excellent." Of Tiberius again he writes, "He never allowed any seed of war to smoulder or kindle into fire either in Greece or in the territory of barbarians, and he bestowed peace and the blessings of peace with rich and bounteous hand and mind upon the whole empire and the whole world[2]." Brutus and his friends could not conceive of this becoming true, and Tacitus too may talk with sovereign pity of the men of his own day who had the misfortune "never to have seen the Republic," but ordinary men, who were not blinded as were Tacitus and the nobles by party-selfishness and by the sense of privileges lost, were well aware that great possibilities of happiness were in store for the world under the young Augustus. And this 'faith' is one key-note of the *Georgics*.

We have therefore no reason to regard Virgil as a mere flatterer, even though in his opening address to Augustus

[1] *Les Latins*, by Édouard Goumy, 1892.
[2] *Legatio ad Caium*, c. XXI.

he may err surprisingly in point of good taste[1]. In that day it was the habit of men, and even of the wisest, to look in Nature for signs of the Divine approval or disapproval. Even in modern days it has been noted that disturbances in Nature often coincide with the loss of great leaders. To the minds of men obsessed by the great career of Julius, by all the good it promised to the world and all that was lost by his death, a great and portentous sign was given. To them the comet which blazed in the heavens during the games held in Caesar's honour after his death was a flaming witness of Heaven's condemnation of his murderers and of his own reception among the deities[2]. And Virgil's actual creed was not so different from that of ordinary men but that he too may have seen in it a solemn message from the powers above. How deep, how passionate was his conviction of the great gift granted to Rome in Julius, of the monstrous sin of the generation who plotted or tolerated his murder, of the Divine wrath as manifested in many a boding portent, is made clear in the conclusion of the first *Georgic*: "The sun out of pity for Rome hides his shining head in murky gloom and a godless generation feared everlasting night in a world where right and wrong are confounded." And he adds with solemn emphasis, *Ergo* "*Therefore it was*, that Romans butchered Romans at Pharsalia and Philippi." And with deep earnestness he prays the Gods of Rome to spare Augustus, "At least permit this youth to come to the succour of a world overthrown. Oh! hinder him

[1] See Sellar's *Virgil*, Ch. VI, 3. Nettleship fixes the composition of *Georgic* I early in B.C. 49. Dio Cassius (LI, 20) tells us that about this time all kinds of public honours were conferred upon Octavian after the settlement of the East, and among others it was decreed that his name should be mentioned in the public forms of worship. Thus about the time when Virgil was writing the *Invocation* the Emperor's fame was being exalted in the name of religion. (*Ancient Lives of Virgil*, p. 58.)

[2] The Caesaris astrum of *Ecl.* IX, 7, the farmer's star under which corn and vines were to prosper: the Julium sidus of Horace, *Odes*, I, 12.

not." 'At least' do not snatch him away like Caesar from a world that so terribly needs him! Every note of sincerity is here.

Such was the birth-time of the *Georgics* at the dawn of the great Roman Revolution. An old world, effete and corrupt, was passing away with violent throes and, amid the hopes and fears of men, a new world was beginning to take its place.

II. PERSONAL

Virgil born and bred in the country. His father and his home. Sainte-Beuve on the influence of his rustic up-bringing. His studies at Rome in rhetoric and philosophy. Siro. He returns home to study and write. His favourite Greek poets. His own early poems. The *Culex*, 'Virgil-ianism.' Virgil the centre of a band of poets, with whom he collaborates. The *Georgics* show great advance on his early work. His dream of art roughly broken. His father's farm confiscated. He has to fly for his life and leaves his native district. Effect of the crisis upon his character and work. A parallel from English Literature.

No one can read a few pages even of the *Georgics* without knowing that Virgil had the good fortune to be born and bred in the country. Everywhere he is recalling the familiar scenes of a happy boyhood spent amid fields and woods, observing and unconsciously chronicling all the sights and sounds around him, familiar with living things, both tame and wild, and all their ways. He knew all the beauty and gladness of what he calls 'the divine country.' It was for him as for our Blackmore a delight to watch the growth and expansion of every green thing. The lines about the shooting of the young vine-branch might for minute observation and sympathy have been written by that great Victorian: "The grasses dare with safety to trust themselves to the spring suns and the young vine-branch has no fear that the south winds will get up or that mighty blasts from the north will hurl down a blast of rain from the sky, but pushes out its buds and unfolds all its leaves[1]." The trees were his friends: for him every different kind had an individuality, and the voice of its rustling sounded as did that of no other: every change that the season brings had its beauty and he touches it with loving hands[2]. Probably the poet's genius could never have developed had he been born and brought up in Rome.

The life of Virgil, long attributed to Donatus, but in reality the work of Suetonius, says that his parents but especially his father were "of humble position." His father was either a potter or the paid servant of some small official of the law-courts, whose son-in-law he became, being commended by his industry. He added to his small means by buying up forest-land and keeping bees, honey being at that time a necessary of life. Evidently he was a man of energy. The hostile critic in Macrobius speaks of Virgil as "a Venetian brought up among woods and thickets"; in the same tone the fellow-artists of the young Millet used to call him "a man of the woods." (There is a legend, unconfirmed, that Virgil's mother, Magia, was a sister of the poet Lucretius[3].) At the age of 12 his father took him to Cremona and seems to have resided with him until his fifteenth birthday, the very day when the poet Lucretius died. From Cremona he passed to Milan and from thence, when he was 16 or 17 years old, to Rome. Probably his father had by this time risen in the world and enlarged his farm, adding field to field, at all events he took pains to give his son

[1] G. II, 331–5: see also 362–6.

[2] See G. II, 398–419, describing how the farmer's operations come round with the changing months, each with its demand of toil and closing with the maxim "Praise a large estate but farm a small one."

[3] It is added in the text of several MSS. of the life of Virgil. The style and language of the Vita are enough to prove unquestionably that it formed one chapter of Suetonius' famous lost book *De Viris Illustribus*. See Nettleship's *Ancient Lives of Virgil*, 1879.

a liberal education; no doubt he realised his talent. Virgil, however, did not, like Horace, study at Athens.

Sainte-Beuve lays stress upon Virgil's origin as son of a small farmer." Such a condition of life," he says, "makes everything better appreciated and more valued...not that the rich cling any less tightly to their vast estates, forests or castles but they cling to them with less of sensibility, in a fashion, than does the poor man or the modest owner of an allotment over which his sweat has dropped, who has counted his vine-stocks and his apple trees and almost reckoned up beforehand even the produce of each. This little domain of Virgil's (perhaps not so small after all) between the hills and the marshes, with its coolness and its springs, its wide pools and its swans, its bees in the willow-hedge, we see it from here, we love it as did he, we cry along with him in the same distress, when he saw himself in peril of losing it, 'Barbarus has segetes!' 'Shall a barbarian become master of fields like these?'"

This fine passage gives one a good notion of the situation of Virgil's early home between the hills and the river, Mincius, which tends to expand into marshes wherever it finds a plain, thus making the climate damp and subject to fogs. Sainte-Beuve is just in emphasising the fact that the crofter watches the welfare of all his crops and cattle more carefully, and anticipates the harvest with far more both of hope and anxiety than does the large farmer. No doubt this helped to produce the homeliness and sympathy with common life which marks Virgil's poetry.

Several of his teachers in Rome we know. One was Parthenius, said to have written the poem translated by Virgil under the title of *Moretum*; it is a description of a countryman, rising at break of day, pulling vegetables in his garden and preparing his breakfast; a charming Dutch picture, full of the enjoyment of homely details. He studied rhetoric under Epidius; the teacher also of the young Octavian, who was some seven years younger than Virgil. It is not impossible that they were pupils at the same time and, though so different in rank, may have been known to each other. Later he studied under the famous Epicurean Siro. In the most interesting of his minor poems, he expresses his contempt for the teachers of rhetoric;

Away with you hence, ye empty swelling phrases of rhetoricians, mere words puffed out, but not with dew from Helicon, ye tribe of pedants, soaking in fat. Get hence, ye empty tinkling cymbals of our youth, and thou, O Sextus Sabinus! my dearest care, farewell; farewell ye goodly youths. I am now setting sail for the blissful haven, seeking the wise words of the great Siro, and I will deliver my life from every care. Away hence, ye Muses, yes, ye too must away, O sweet Muses! for I will confess the truth, sweet have ye been. And yet I ask you, visit my studies again, though seldom and without wantonness.

It would seem that Virgil left Rome with a certain dis-enchantment, although he was deeply impressed by the teaching of Siro. Evidently the professional scholars of that day tended towards the same faults as do those of our own. These very fresh and spontaneous lines show a profound contempt for mere learning and intellectual pretentiousness, as well as a determination, not shared by most young poets, to come into touch with the reality of things by means of philosophy. They show also his keen delight in poetry, his affection for his fellow-students and his distaste for the licentious tone common in the poetry of his day. If the Roman litterateurs disappointed Virgil, the teaching of Siro impressed him deeply. Siro belonged to that noble class of Epicureans, who followed closely in their master's footsteps and of whom Cicero speaks so highly. Epicurus' strong advocacy of tem-perance and the simple life, his earnest warnings against ambition and his deep sympathy with the poor and the ignorant must have commended him deeply to Virgil, both in his youth and always. At the same time Epicureanism as a system could be no abiding-place for a spirit so broad and well-balanced as Virgil's. In his early years he admired it for its attempt to solve the problems of natural science though he soon recognised that this was not his own province. Grand as was the gain of a reign of law

established in Nature Virgil ere long came to feel that
there were many problems which Epicurean science, with
all its dogmatic pretensions, was helpless to explain. What
of the origin of life? What of the facts of our self-con-
sciousness? The world was too big a world, and Lucretius'
solution of it far too complete ever to satisfy a mind like
his.

The young poet must have been glad to return to Andes.
As years went on his father grew blind. No doubt Virgil
assisted him in managing his farm. At the same time he
was busy studying and writing. We imagine him reading
Homer and Theocritus under the shadow of some mighty
beech or by the side of a stream, never yet realizing that
he was himself to become one of the world's great poets.
How completely he assimilated Homer the whole plot and
action of the *Aeneid* shows. Probably he did not become
a student of the great Athenian dramas until later years.
His first poems, the *Eclogues*, are manifestly the work of
one who "lives" in the study of literature, assimilating
in ample leisure the poets whom he loves. He trained
himself after the noble models of Greece, not excluding
the Alexandrians, whom the young writers of his
day generally imitated. But Virgil's passionate love
for Lucretius made him proof against their sickly seduc-
tions, with all their erudition and their pretty and laboured
pictures, which do not grow organically out of the subject.
As Sainte-Beuve says of Apollonius Rhodius, such poets
"made no hearts beat." Virgil knew this well. In the
opening of *Georgic* III, he refers to the myths which the
Alexandrians and his own Roman contemporaries loved
to treat as subjects "which could once have captivated
idle minds[1]," but which were now impossible for himself.
Not improbably he was thinking of the *Culex* with its
catalogue of mythological lay figures.

One main feature of Virgil's work as a poet is the steady
growth and advance which it shows. In the *Eclogues* he
imitates a true poet, Theocritus. Theocritus is more real:

[1] Cetera quae vacuas tenuissent carmina mentes, *G.* III, 3.

his shepherds are drawn from life; but Virgil has trans-
muted the *Idyll* of Theocritus and made of it a new poetic
form: his shepherds are also friends of his own, who, under
this disguise, set forth their own troubles and loves. This,
though graceful, is no doubt a very artificial kind of
poetry, but *Colin Clout's Calendar* and *Lycidas* show how
much of genuine feeling it can be made to hold. Virgil
was well aware of its artificiality. At the close of the
Georgics he says, looking back to his *Eclogues*: "Once I
played with shepherd's songs[1]"; and also of the poem he
had just completed: "Such was the song I was making of
the tending of fields and cattle and of trees, while Caesar,
that mighty one, is hurling war's lightnings over deep
Euphrates and imposing statutes upon the willing nations.
At that time I was being nursed in the sweet lap of Naples,
treading the flowery ways of inglorious ease." Surely these
words are most unjust to that noble poem the *Georgics*!
But Virgil felt that the poet's mission was to deal with
the whole of human life, not merely with that spent amid
the quiet of the country that he loved so well. These
concluding words prepare us for the opening of his great
poem, "Arms and the man I sing—a man made exile
by destiny, much buffeted on land and on the deep by
violence from the gods and much scourged in war, him
from whom sprang the Latin people and the towering
walls of Rome." His theme is now the story of the whole
Roman nation bound up with that of a man who had to
battle with all the forces of destiny banded against him
as well as with his own human weakness, who, conquering at last, reached a home and abiding-place for
himself and his people. With this lifelong aspiration and
striving after growth we can understand his final charge
to his friends, Varius and Tucca, when, just before his
death, he forbade them to publish anything which he had
not himself included in his published works.

The *Georgics* were composed during Virgil's prime,

---

[1] Carmina qui lusi pastorum, *G.* IV, 565. See note.

between his thirty-third and fortieth years[1]. Probably the *Aeneid* was planned (set forth in prose first of all, as Suetonius tells us) and much of it written during the same period. A number of poems are attributed to Virgil, which are not included in his published works. These used to be looked upon as spurious. Of late they have been much studied, and many scholars now consider several of the shorter ones to be genuine early work of Virgil's. Dr Warde Fowler and Professor R. S. Conway regard the *Culex* also, a poem of over 400 lines, as a work of his youth[2]. All these poems are full of what seem, at first, to be echoes or imitations of Virgil's accepted writings; but when compared with the latter, they impress us not as derived from these but as expressing the same thoughts and emotions in a feebler and undeveloped form, as if he had returned in later life to the same notes of thought and feeling which had attracted him in youth, and now expressed them more forcibly. We know that Virgil collaborated with other poets, notably with Gallus[3]. Mackail says that "the two poets worked at their art together," and he compares this joint literary activity to that of Spenser and Sidney, or that of Wordsworth and Coleridge. One of the parallel passages occurs at *Georgic* II, 458–74,

O fortunatos nimium, sua si bona norint, | Agricolas!

Both in thought and treatment this reproduces *Culex*, 58–78, beginning "O bona pastoris." Both deal with the joys of the Simple Life and the original inspiration of both is in the opening of Lucretius' Second Book. But the

[1] In *G.* II, 163, Virgil refers to the double Julian harbour constructed by Agrippa in B.C. 37. The completed poem was read to Augustus after his final return from the East in 29. Various passages with historical references were probably inserted after the poem was composed.

[2] See *Class. Review*, 1914, p. 119.

[3] Thus the closing four lines of the long poem, *Ciris*, now generally attributed to Gallus, recur verbatim at *G.* I, 406–9, where see note.

poet of the *Culex* is no mere imitator of the passage in the *Georgic*: he has a voice of his own. Suetonius says that Virgil wrote the *Culex* at the age of sixteen.

Saturated as Virgil's mind was in youth with the Greek poets, he came as we shall see under another influence more mighty still, that of Lucretius. The leaven of Lucretius worked on his heart all his life through. In those early years the young poet was training himself in the mastery of his craft, acquiring the exquisite command over expression and verse which is seen in the *Eclogues*. So consummate is his skill that the pleasure of reading these is like that of sipping some exquisite wine or enjoying the scent of some rich flower: as Tennyson puts it:

> All the charm of all the Muses
> Often flowering in a lonely word.

Thus his youth was passed in a dream of art, a peaceful existence in which the stern facts of life are known merely from books, as of one who watches the movements in a street from a mirror inside his room. Those who follow such pursuits are apt to drop out of touch with ordinary men struggling in the great world outside their own little circle. But it was not to be so with Virgil. The great forces which were then shaping the destiny of Rome were to come into rude collision with his own too safe and quiet life.

Virgil's acquaintance with all the details of country life and farm-work is so full and so tinged with his own personality that it must have been acquired through assisting his father on his farm. He writes of the operations of planting, pruning, grafting with the delight of one who has put his own hand to the work. In the ninth *Eclogue* the land of Menalcas (who stands for Virgil) is described thus: "I had heard that all the land from where the hills begin to draw themselves up and to send down a ridge with gentle slope on to the water and the old beeches with broken tops, your Menalcas had saved by his songs." The lines seem to give a real picture of Virgil's farm as it dwelt in his memory and affection. Doubtless he loved every field there and many a fancy of his hung round those tempest-shattered beeches which marked the boundary. (The passage has been thought to imply a considerable stretch of land but, until we know the exact position of Andes, we cannot be certain as to this.) The tone of the *Georgics* however does not suggest that Virgil had ever himself spent whole days in ploughing, sowing or reaping as did Robert Burns or the great painter who received his first inspiration from Virgil, Jean François Millet[1].

In the year after the battle of Philippi when Virgil had reached the age of twenty-nine the territory of Cremona and part of the Mantuan was confiscated. The soldier to whom the farm of Virgil's father had been allotted threatened the poet's life and he had to escape by swimming the river Mincius. His father had become blind and a home had to be found for him; in a poem of a few lines Virgil tells us where.

O cottage that once was Siro's and thou, poor little croft! yet even thou wast as good as wealth to an owner such as he, to thee, if I hear ought gloomier news about my native place, I entrust myself and along with thee, those whom I have always loved and foremost of all my father. To him thou shalt now be what Mantua and Cremona had beforetime been.

Virgil seems never to have returned to his native region: probably the mosquito-haunted Mantuan district with its lagoons[2] did not suit health like his. He went up to Rome, where his first poems found great favour with Augustus. The emperor, himself fond of writing, presented him at different periods with valuable estates near Naples and in Sicily. The poet tells us that it was in the district of

---

[1] "Virgil," says Sensier, "charmed Millet so much when a boy that he could not stop reading him. The *Bucolics* and *Georgics* captivated his mind. At the words of Virgil 'It is the hour when the great shadows descend towards the plain,' the child was filled with emotion: the book recalled to him his own surroundings, the life in which he was growing up."

[2] The subject of the *Culex* or 'Gnat' may thus have been suggested.

Naples that the *Georgics* were composed. Augustus also offered him the estate of some banished man, but this, Suetonius tells us, the poet "could not endure to accept," *non sustinuit accipere*. This rude experience of insecurity and danger seems to have had a profound influence upon Virgil. When we compare the *Georgics* with his early poems, the *Eclogues*, a great difference appears. Instead of dialogues of make-believe shepherds, we have passed into a real world of actual men, the same world of labour and toil in which we live and struggle to-day. He is now no longer "playing with shepherds' songs." His own harsh experiences seem to have deepened his sympathy with all the suffering of the world from whatever source it may come.

There is a parallel to this in English literature. The poet Wordsworth was profoundly attached to his brother John, who was captain of an East Indiaman. He was making his last voyage before retiring to live at Grasmere, when his vessel was sunk during a hurricane in the Bristol Channel, almost in sight of land. The poet describes how, after this, a great change passed over himself: he paid more heed to the actual world, to the men and women whom he was meeting every day. In a very beautiful poem entitled *Elegiac verses written on a picture of Peele Castle in a storm* he describes the change thus wrought. The picture represented an old castle on a cliff with the sea in a tempest and a disabled ship drifting on to the rocks. Wordsworth had lived near it in calm weather when the castle was always reflected in the waves and one could have fancied the sea the gentlest among all gentle things. Had he been a painter, he would then have painted it in full sunshine with the sea sleeping at its feet.

> Such, in the fond illusion of·my heart,
> Such Picture would I at that time have made:...

> So once it would have been,—'tis so no more;
> I have submitted to a new control:
> A power is gone which nothing can restore;
> A deep distress hath humanised my Soul.

He now commends the painter because he has chosen to represent the castle in storm:

> This work of thine I blame not, but commend;
> This sea in anger, and that dismal shore....
>
> O 'tis a passionate Work!—yet wise and well,
> Well chosen is the spirit that is here;
> That hulk which labours in the deadly swell,
> This rueful sky, this pageantry of fear!
>
> Farewell, farewell the heart that lives alone,
> Housed in a dream, at distance from the Kind!
> Such happiness, wherever it be known,
> Is to be pitied; for 'tis surely blind.

Some influence like this seems to have passed over Virgil: his forcible expulsion from his old home along with his neighbours, also exiled to wander homeless: his narrow escape with his life, all this seems to have created in him or rather to have intensified his sympathy with all human hardship and peril. Thus the *Georgics* show his profound fellow-feeling with all who suffer from war as well as with those who have to toil for the bare necessaries of living. One might point to his picture in the *Aeneid* of the emigrants, storm-tossed and sea-weary, hating to think that they must again cross the ocean from which they have just escaped and now shudder at the very sight of, sick with hopeless longing for some home in the unknown land they seek. His heart is now in touch with all human experience.

III. VIRGIL'S ATTITUDE TO ETHICS AND RELIGION IN THE *GEORGICS*

The poem as a manual of Husbandry. Agriculture destroyed by the Civil Wars. Degeneration of the Roman character. Sense of guilt in the Nation. Virgil counsels his countrymen to restore Agriculture as the basis of recovery. His practical Philosophy. The Dignity of Labour; its necessity for man. Providence has ordained in kindness that the husbandman's life should be hard. The husbandman's work more than any other man's brings him into touch with the Divine Power behind Nature. Influence of Lucretius in the *Georgics*. Two sides of Lucretius' Poem. I. His science, which Virgil admires but only very partially mastered. Virgil's strange inconsistency here. He is more of a Lucretian than an Epicurean. II. Lucretius' passionate pity for mankind, his sense of the nothingness of man in the Universe yet of the Dignity of his Spirit, also of the marvellous beauty of the Earth. On this side Lucretius' influence over Virgil was life-long and enriched his humanity. Virgil outgrows Lucretius' influence in the former case. He makes no attempt to reconcile his Epicurean science with his attitude to national and personal religion. Constant advance and growth in Virgil's thought and art.

The *Georgics* have a two-fold aspect. The poem professes to be a treatise on Husbandry and it is also a great work of literature. In the first respect it shows an intimate and practical knowledge of the whole subject which could only have been acquired by personal experience. Virgil also uses well-known authorities on agriculture such as Varro, *De Re Rustica* (published just before he began to write his poem), especially in the third and fourth *Georgics* treating of cattle-breeding and bee-farming, also Xenophon's *Oeconomicus* as to soils, ploughing, sowing and so on. He is also acquainted, probably not directly, with Aristotle's *History of Animals*, and he uses Aratus' poems on *Weather-signs* and other works. The poem was accepted as a practical and standard manual upon the subject, for example by Columella who wrote on agriculture about

A.D. 60. Even on this practical side the book is a labour of love. It is worth noting that Virgil recommends, as a principle taken for granted in his day, the alternation of crops: the farmer should allow the land to produce and lie fallow by turns: he must let grain alternate with beans, vetches and lupines: either plan will give 'rest' to the fields. The rotation of crops is now an established rule in Britain but was not so until well into the 18th century. In so far Roman husbandry was for long in advance of our own.

When we consider the state of husbandry in Italy while the *Georgics* were being written, we cannot wonder that Maecenas suggested this subject to Virgil or at least strongly encouraged him to write upon it. During a long period of civil wars, agriculture had been neglected, so much so indeed that an impression had spread that the earth had become less fertile because the world had reached its extreme old age and would soon come to an end. Lucretius in the end of his second book puts this feeling in the mouth of the aged ploughman lamenting over the rich produce of old days, although the former holdings were far smaller than the present ones while "the planter of the exhausted and shrivelled vine sadly cries out upon the changes in the seasons, and wearies Heaven with his prayers, and understands not that all things are wasting away little by little, and are passing to the grave, spent and worn out by age and length of years."

The facts of barrenness and decay were plain enough. But Lucretius misread them. He forgot that the strong arms which had tilled the soil, once so prolific, were mouldering on many a battlefield. Many districts were going back to the waste. The independent peasantry who had been the most valuable class of the community were rapidly disappearing. The fashion of *latifundia*, 'big estates,' had come in. Wealthy absentee owners had bought up the farms at nominal prices and had them cultivated by gangs of slaves, with whom owing to the Roman conquests the markets were flooded. These had multiplied enormously while the few peasants were becoming extinct and what was left of them were crowding into the towns and degenerating. What wonder that the fields had become less fertile? The gloomy fancy of a dying Earth shows what a strain those long years of civil war had left on the nerves and mind of Virgil's generation.

We must remember that between the life-time of Virgil and the days of the old 'Commonwealth,' the Respublica—before that great name had been debased and its powers usurped by the Senate—the Roman nation had undergone great changes. Rome had become mistress of all the countries round the Mediterranean, and the Romans gathered into their hands the trade and commerce of that vast territory. The nation had become enormously wealthy and wealth brought new temptations with it. Their ancestors used to set a great value on truth and honour; they despised, even refused to tolerate, luxurious living or extravagance. But the old ideals of honour, plain-living and simplicity had in great part passed away. Wealth was sought after by any means. Instead of being incorruptible Roman juries were now willing to give unjust decisions if a big enough bribe could be paid. Governors went out to their provinces poor and returned with fortunes. Roman Senators were in collusion with the pirates and shared their gains. The story of Cluentius whom Cicero defended in the year 66 B.C. shows how bold then was the criminal, how openly unjust the judge, how little chance of safety had the innocent.

Augustus and his Prime Minister, Maecenas, were far too shrewd not to realize the vital importance of restoring the *coloni* or crofters and securing their rights to the land. Both recognised the renewing of the old Italian prestige in agriculture as the basis of national prosperity. Virgil, addressing Maecenas, speaks of his suggestion as "thy behest and no light one[1]." No subject could have been more in touch with his sympathies, as Maecenas doubtless knew. The poem is didactic, full of good judgment in accordance with the best science of the time tested by his

[1] Tua, Maecenas, haud mollia iussa. *G.* III, 41.

own experience. But Virgil always knows how to sub-ordinate this to the living interest of the theme. His ideals of human life had been vividly quickened by the great national crisis which he had lived through. Beyond question the murder of Caesar and the events leading up to the battles of Philippi and Actium pervaded his whole horizon and stimulated his own convictions, even as the character and beliefs of our own Spenser were moulded by the Bartholomew massacre, the assassination of William the Silent and the defeat of the Spanish Armada.

The ideals of the time Virgil felt to be false and un-natural. They had caused infinite bloodshed, poverty and suffering. At thought of them Virgil was moved as was Jeanne D'Arc by "the great pity that was in France." There rose before him the picture of a better national life for his own country, a life happier and more human, which he has set forth for all time in the *Georgics*.

Men who loved their country like Virgil, were distressed to see the old standards degenerating. Especially in Rome, though he admired it and calls it the most beautiful thing on earth, the sense of this forced itself upon him. To a nature like his the misery of the poor crowded away in the many-storied *insulae* or 'blocks' of the city and the lavish luxury of the rich were alike revolting. There is a deep note of sincerity in his protest.

"Men have ceased," he says, "to distinguish right from wrong: their lives are dominated by ambition, by the greed for power and luxury and the passion for artificial pleasures. In pursuit of these no guilt or treachery whether to the State or to kindred or friends appals them. The world is covered with wars; cities are sacked and houses destroyed for mere greed of booty and every form of crime abounds. The labour of the farmer is no longer held in honour. Men have grown out of touch with Nature. Yet in the country even now religion survives, age is honoured, the youth are strong to labour and inured to hard-ship and Justice may still be found[1]."

---

[1] These sentences give the main drift of *Georgic* I, 501 ff. and II, 495–512. Note such phrases as impia saecula, I, 468; fas versum atque nefas, 505; Mars impius, 511.

There was in the nation at this time a widespread feeling that Rome was now paying for the crime of her foremost citizens who had sacrificed their country to their ambition. Dr Warde Fowler speaks of

"the gloom that overspread all classes especially after the assassination of the Dictator." "Caesar," he says, "seemed irresistible and godlike, and men were probably beginning to hope for some new and more stable order of things when he was suddenly struck down, and the world plunged again into confusion and doubt; and it was not till after the final victory of Octavian at Actium, and the destruction of the elements of disunion with the deaths of Antony and Cleopatra, that men really began to hope for better times. The literature of those melancholy years shows distinct signs of the general depression, which was perhaps something more than weariness and material discomfort; there was almost what we may call a dim sense of sin, or at least of moral evil, such a feeling, though far less real and intense, as that which their prophets aroused from time to time in the Jewish people and one not unknown in the history of Hellas[1]."

So too Professor Conway finds in Virgil

the conscious possession of an idea that the guilt of mankind had grown to be unendurable so that the world was pitiably in need of regeneration;

and he adds,

No one who is even superficially acquainted with the terrible century before Augustus (say from 133–31 B.C.) will doubt that the sufferings caused to the world by the 'delirium' of its rulers had reached an unbearable pitch. In that period of time Italy had seen twelve separate civil wars, six of which had involved many of the provinces; a long series of political murders, beginning with the Gracchi, and ending with Caesar and Cicero[2].

Thus even Horace in his 16th *Epode* complains that his country which no enemy could conquer is being destroyed in the Civil Wars by its own strength, and proposes that Romans should abandon their own land and found a new and better Rome in the islands of the West. There may

---

[1] *Social Life in the age of Cicero*, p. 349.
[2] *Virgil's Messianic Eclogue*, 1907, pp. 31–33.

be little sincerity here but he expresses the general dis-heartenment of the Romans of his day. How poorly does this " counsel of despair," this childish dream of the Roman people abandoning their country, contrast with the noble patriotism of the *Georgics*! Virgil reminds his country-men that the nation may yet be saved from its guilt and ruin, if they will cast away their false ambitions, revive the old pride in their beautiful home-land and take up afresh the industry of the fields which lie waste or neglected.

Virgil realizes perhaps as strongly as does Thomas Carlyle the dignity of work and its necessity for the very soul of man : both would have agreed that all work brings hope and courage with it, and that it alone gives dignity to human life. The whole of the *Georgics* show how profoundly he had been impressed by Lucretius' con-ception of the hard and unequal struggle which man has to wage with unsympathetic and reluctant Nature in order to maintain his existence. It is a dark picture. But Virgil views this struggle from a very different standpoint. To him Nature is not independent in her own sphere. As Sellar has well said,

The Lucretian conception of Nature in its relation to human wants has been greatly modified by the religious tendency of Virgil's thought, his respect for traditional opinion, his sense of man's dependence on a higher Spiritual Power[1].

Throughout the poem he names this supreme Power, *Pater*, ' The Father,' while Lucretius finds in Nature no smallest regard for man. Virgil expresses his own thought here by re-casting the old myth about the passing of the Golden Age when Jupiter deprived man of fire and forbade the earth to bear harvests untilled, and gave poison to snakes and sent the wolf prowling and made the sea breed storms. This was not done out of enmity to man. No! "The Father himself has willed that the farmer's path be no easy one[2]," his crops are ever in danger. But Jupiter

---

[1] *Virgil*, Chap. VI, § 2.   [2] *G.* I, 121.

has set signs in the heavens to guide him, constellations whose rise and setting show him at what seasons to plough and sow. The farmer must watch these as closely as does the sailor; other signs are given him in the air or on the earth from the aspects of sun and moon and sky, the behaviour of beasts, of birds or even insects to warn him of drought and rain and tempest, or extremes of heat or cold. All these the Father has ordained as "infallible tokens[1]" for the husbandman's guidance. "Never was man surprised by rain unawares." By this constant need for wariness, alertness and effort man has developed and grown in faculty and character and found out for himself the various arts of civilisation. Were it not for this, he would have lived in sloth and remained on the level of the brutes. "Thus toil conquered all difficulties, relentless Toil and Want that grinds men in adversity."

But the husbandman has more enemies than the weather. There is a tendency in all things to change for the worse. Unless year by year the seeds of his crops are inspected and he carefully chooses out the best and largest, the quality of every plant is sure to degenerate: "all earthly things are doomed to fall away to the worse and to slide back and deteriorate, as with a rower who just manages to make head against the stream: if once he relax his arms, the current whirls his boat away down the river[2]."

It is the pride of the husbandman that by constant labour and watchfulness he can counteract these dangers and hold his own. Thus he wins what Virgil calls "the glory of the divine country[3]," and is able to "lay his commands on the fields" which are his kingdom[4].

But there is another aspect of the farmer's work which commends it to the poet. He holds that it, more than any other form of toil, brings man into touch with the Spiritual Power behind Nature, not merely because he more than others is dependent on that living force which may either wreck or foster the labour of his hands, but because those

[1] G. I, 351.   [2] G. I, 200.
[3] G. I, 168.   [4] Imperat arvis, G. I, 99.

whose lives are spent like his in immediate contact with
Nature feel the Divine Power to be nearer to them than
do those who live in cities. Not in didactic form or
specific statement, but in one way or other every great
poem is found to express some theory of man's life in
relation to the universe. Evidently Lucretius' statement
of Law in Nature was to Virgil a revelation which brought
order to his mind where before had been confusion. Yet
he holds the doctrine with strange inconsistency. In the
same passage we find the belief in Divine interposition
in Nature side by side with verses accepting the belief in
natural law. Thus, in explaining how the farmer must
study the different qualities of different soils and cannot
hope for success without applying the proper treatment
to each, he says:

Such is the chain of law, such the eternal covenants which
Nature has imposed on given climates ever since the day when
Deucalion first hurled stones on the unpeopled earth, stones
whence sprung men, a race hard as they.

> Continuo has leges aeternaque foedera certis
> Imposuit natura locis, quo tempore primum
> Deucalion, etc.[1]

Here is the plainest admission of the reign of law, yet
close upon it treads a reference to the old myths of
Deucalion and Pyrrha who created the human race by
throwing behind their backs stones which turned into
men and women. Strange to say the same inconsistency
recurs in the 6th *Eclogue* where Silenus sings how the
world and living things came into being from atoms
jostling in the void and passes at once from this to tell
of the stones that Pyrrha threw, the childish marvel-
legend handed down from some prehistoric race. Such a
juxtaposition of new science and old mythology would be
impossible for any one who thoroughly realized Epicurus'
great doctrine. The gifted French critic, Emile Faguet,
says of the latter passage that "it is far more Lucretian
than Epicurean." (The same phrase may still better be

[1] *G.* I, 60.

applied to Virgil himself.) Faguet remarks that the passage last named is

too close a textual imitation of Lucretius not to show that Virgil is following an author whom he has just read without making any advance upon him, without combining him with anything else or with his (Virgil's) own thought, timidly and not letting go the handrail. like one who is on a staircase absolutely unknown to him[1].

The poem of Lucretius contains two things, first an admirably clear and exact account of Epicurean science and doctrine: the other is what Lucretius has added out of his own heart and imagination to Epicurus' teaching. The influence of the former over Virgil has been greatly over-stated: probably he never had any real grasp of Epicurean science although he has a genuine admiration for these early attempts to explain the phenomena of Nature, a task for which he says that others are better fitted than himself. One may doubt if he ever mastered the atomic theory, so admirably expounded by Lucretius. Poetic sensibility—and few have more of that than Virgil —is not often accompanied by real scientific bent. Virgil has been charged with great inconsistency because of two successive sentences in the second *Georgic*[2]. He extols Lucretius because of the deliverance he has wrought for mankind, "Happy is he who had the power to learn the causes of things, and so trampled underfoot all manner of fears (meaning superstitious fears) and relentless death and the roar of insatiate Acheron[3]." Yet while extolling he does not accept the doctrines (for example that of annihilation at death) on which Lucretius bases this deliverance. What follows these words? "Blessed is he who has won the friendship of the gods of the country, Pan and old Silvanus and the sisterhood of the Nymphs." Yet how reconcile the former thanksgiving, possible only

[1] *Cosmopolis*, July, 1897.
[2] *G.* II, 490-5.
[3] The roaring of the infernal river symbolises the appalling-ness of ever-devouring death.

because the Gods have no power on earth for good or ill, with this admiration for the man who knows the Gods of the country and their benign influence?

The inconsistency is glaring, but I believe Virgil intended it to be so. The dilemma must not be pressed too closely. Some minds can, especially in youth, hold by two conflicting points of view because they feel there is truth in both and have no overpowering, inner sense of compulsion to reconcile the two. For others again such an attitude is impossible.

Again nothing could well be more antagonistic to the Epicurean creed than the lines in the fourth *Georgic*[1] where Virgil sets forth his own belief in the Stoic doctrine that God pervades the whole of Nature, earth, ocean and heaven, that from Him men and all living things derive the breath of life, and that the life which came from Him must return to its source on high; thus "there is no room for death." In the speech of Anchises in the sixth *Aeneid* the same doctrine recurs but there it is more developed and it has a strong Platonic tinge: in the soul there is a Divine element akin to aether, which is the cause of all our aspirations after goodness and according as we live well or ill remains bright or becomes clogged, so that a Purgatory after death is needed to restore its purity. (The doctrine in this later form is strongly ethical. The contrast between the two passages illustrates the constant growth and clearing in Virgil's thought as in his art. The Pantheistic deity of the *Georgics* who is the source of all life but takes no side with good against evil is a philosophical rather than a religious conception.) The doctrine of the Anima Mundi or 'Soul of the World,' which Epicurus so strongly combated, reminds us that even in the *Georgics* Virgil cannot really be called an Epicurean. How very much less so in the *Aeneid*! Perhaps indeed Virgil never comes so much in harmony with Epicurean teaching as when he is contrasting the anxious ever-agitated career of ambition or the life of luxury and its

[1] *G.* IV, 219-227.

constant craving for pleasure with the peacefulness and dignity of the Simple Life[1]. Here Virgil and Lucretius are entirely in accord.

But Lucretius' poem has another side which, though it was the outcome of Epicurean science working in the poet's own soul and imagination, was not of Epicurus;— he indeed would have refused to consider it. Lucretius' conviction that man is merely the creation of the blindly-jostling atoms, helped to force on Virgil a sense of man's nothingness in an infinite universe, yet also of the dignity of his spirit, while at the same time the beauty of the world became touched with grandeur as the scene of man's unequal struggle with destiny. The contrast between the human lives, frail but indomitable, which are being played out on the precarious stage of earth amid awful forces that reck nought of man is never far away in Lucretius' poem: this makes it more tender and more human. In defiance of his creed the world which Epicurus held to be a dead machine remains to Lucretius Divine and full of mystery. His passion of pity for the strange destiny of man and his reverential sense of the marvellous beauty of the earth, made every fibre of the young Virgil's heart to throb, long after he had ceased to be of Epicurus' school. The influence was life-long. Had Lucretius never written, Virgil would have missed something of the deep and rich humanity which has made him one of the world's best-loved teachers.

Born and bred in the country, Virgil had been familiar from boyhood with the rites of the old Italian worship of the Gods of field and fold. He had a compelling sense that the worshippers and he himself were thus brought into touch with a Power outside themselves, by whatever name they might address it. There are certain natures to which the sight of the swelling buds, the springing corn, the blossoming tree, brings a profound sense of the Divine, of what a great man of science has called "the beautiful but awful Omnipresence which every flower and every

[1] As in *G*. II, 458 to the close.

insect reveals[1]." When Virgil speaks of "the divine country[2]," he means that the Gods are specially near there. Of no other poet could it be said with more truth than of Virgil that his days were "bound each to each by natural piety." By native temperament he was deeply sensitive to all those influences of the outer world which bring home to us the sense of a great Life behind all the shows of Nature. This conviction carried with it a deep-rooted sense of reality. To this Virgil's steadfast nature clung: the philosophers with all their arguments could not shake it. He listened to them but he could not be deaf to that other voice which spoke out of the depth of his heart. Nor could he forget that the rustic worshippers with their simple faith had been in the past and still were nobler men than the cultured folk who denied the Gods and despised their worship, more patriotic, more modest, more sincere. He would not attempt to reconcile the new science with the conviction that was bound up with his earliest experience. In a world full of so many things which he could not explain, he would keep his mind open to both points of view, and wait until more light came. By the time when his great sixth *Aeneid* was written, a new teacher, Plato, had for him supplanted Epicurus in all the deeper matters of belief[3].

[1] Professor Kitchen Parker.   [2] *G.* I, 168.
[3] One version of Donatus' life concludes by observing that although the opinions of various philosophers may be found in Virgil's poems, he was a Platonist, ipse tamen fuit Academicus. Nam Platonis sententias omnibus aliis praetulit. (From the *Life* prefixed to the Delphine edition.)

IV. VIRGIL'S BORROWINGS: HIS STYLE, METRE; AIM OF THE POEM

Virgil's literary epithets are never found in Lucretius. He makes his borrowings his own and new. Change in the plan of the fourth *Georgic*. The simple and the elaborate style in poetry: Virgil's not simple. No poet so much quoted. Why? His metrical effects as compared with those of Milton and Tennyson. Sainte-Beuve's canon that "every true poem of any length must be grafted into its own age by applying some main events of the poet's time." This canon fulfilled in the *Georgics*. Virgil's world out of joint. Central idea of the Poem.

The *Georgics*, though professing to be a didactic poem, is far more than this. Virgil handles each point of his subject with illustration and circumstances so well selected that it appeals not only to our heart and imagination but also to our sense of beauty. It is a true work of art. Ploughing and sowing, grafting and vine pruning, weather-signs, cattle and the ways of bees all provide him with pictures bright and genial and rich in human associations[1]. Comparing Millet's *Angelus* and Virgil's poem Mr T. E. Page has well said, "The art which from two peasants, a potato field and a church spire in the distance can create a great picture is strictly parallel with the art which Virgil exhibits in the *Georgics*[2]."

A reader who might take the poem up without any previous knowledge of Augustan literature could not fail to be struck by the constant references to Greek literature and Greek associations of places and things. "Sometimes," says Sidgwick, "this is done with a mere epithet: the 'Chaonian' acorn, the 'Lethean' poppy, the 'Acheloian' cups of water, the 'Paphian' myrtle, 'Amyclean' dogs, 'Cretan' quiver, the 'Idaean' pitch, 'Cecropian' bees." So also the frequent references to Ariadne, Procne, Scylla, Parnassus, Helicon, etc. "If the poet mentions water-

---

[1] See the instances cited by Sellar, Chap. VI, §2.
[2] Edition of *Virgil*, Vol. I, p. 23.

birds, they 'sport round Caystrian pools in the Asian
meads,' an orchard reminds him of 'the groves of Alcinous,'
the lightning strikes Athos or Rhodope or the Ceraunian
rocks'' and so on[1]. Not only Virgil but every man of any
culture in Rome was familiar with Homer and the other
Greek poets and he expresses himself in terms of these.
In *Georgic* IV he transfers to his poem from the *Odyssey*
the charming Sea-myth of Proteus, adapting it to his
purpose.

Could we imagine Lucretius using 'literary epithets'
such as those just quoted? They are artificial, because
they make the poetry of a thing to consist in its
associations more than in the thing itself: they are
absolutely alien to the direct strength of Virgil's poetic
master.

Probably no great poet ever owed so much to preceding ones as did Virgil. But he has an extraordinary
power to make his own what he borrows and to present
it in new aspects and with widened significance. I may
refer to two similes in the sixth *Aeneid*, the comparison
of the form of Dido dimly seen among the ghosts to the
moon which one "sees or fancies he has seen" among the
clouds when the month is new, and to that other where
the spirits crowding down to the bank of Styx are
compared to the withered leaves that flutter and fall in
the first frost of autumn. The originals are to be found
in the poem of Apollonius of Rhodes, each of about a line
and a half, but in each case this brief reference is by Virgil
widened and ennobled into an altogether new poetic
content[2].

The latter half of the fourth *Georgic* is puzzling. After
assuring the reader that he will not detain him with re-
telling old myths, or with circuitous treatment of any
kind[3], Virgil closes the poem with a long episode which has

[1] Sidgwick. Introduction, Vol. I, p. 34.
[2] Both instances are excellently discussed by Professor
R. Y. Tyrrell, *Lectures on Latin Poetry*, 1895, p. 142.
[3] *G.* II, 46.

nothing to do with Italy and almost nothing, in a strict sense, to do with country-life. Even were there no tradition that Augustus demanded the omission of the story of Gallus, any one who is familiar with Virgil's treatment in the rest of the poem, could hardly fail to infer that this concluding part was a later substitution, quite different from his original plan. He fails in his attempts to make it relevant but it contains some of his finest writing. How nobly does he here express his deep sense of the tragedy of human love and loss in Eurydice's last words to her husband while he clutches vainly at her form as she is swept away amid the darkness—

> Iamque vale: feror ingenti circumdata nocte.

Who could ever translate this line[1]?

In poetry there is room for more styles than one, just as in dress: there is a charm in simple dress and also in rich so long as both are in good taste. One would not wish every poet to be as unadorned in style as Wordsworth.

As an instance of an absolutely direct and simple style one might name that old Scottish Ballad of *The Twa Corbies*,

> As I was walking all alane
> I heard twa corbies making a maen.
> The tane unto the t'other gan say
> "Whaur sall we gang and dine to-day?
>
> "In behint yon auld fail[2] dyke
> I wot there lies a new-slain knight,
> And naebody kens that he lies there
> But his hawk, his hound, and his lady faire....

concluding thus

> "O'er his white banes when they are bare,
> The wind sall blaw for evermair."

[1] In lines like this and "sunt lacrimae rerum" does not the very simplicity of the expression help to make rendering so very difficult?

[2] Turf.

The least cultured person could understand every line of this while the person of most culture would alike feel what the nameless genius in some Border glen who wrote it felt and meant. How it comes home in its simplicity!— the Knight beset and slain while at his sport through the treachery of the woman he loves[1]!

There is no question that Virgil's style is not simple. We might compare it to that of Tennyson which it resembles very closely. It is too condensed, too elaborated to be called simple. Yet this is consistent with a marvellous power and expressiveness. Take for instance one line which has always appeared to me very Virgilian, not indeed Virgilian in the best sense but in that of being somewhat artificial and yet powerful by reason of its very art. It is in Tennyson's *Dream of fair women*. Iphigenia is on the point of being sacrificed to appease the anger of Artemis. The priest is actually raising the knife to slay her when the goddess takes pity and carries her off in a cloud. Iphigenia speaks,

> The bright death quivered at the victim's throat,
> Touched and I knew no more.

That is not a direct use of language. You could not imagine the poet of *The Twa Corbies* using such a phrase. Try to do so: you feel you could not, yet how vivid it is! Virgil's style is not simple in point of language but in thought and feeling he is perfectly natural and simple. The same is true of Tennyson.

Probably from the time of Augustine down to Louis Stevenson, whether in books or in the debates of statesmen, no other poet has ever been so much quoted as Virgil. This is due to his wide and profound sympathy with human beings in all conditions and situations of life, the sympathy of a high and generous spirit that savours more of Christian than of Pagan times. He feels and makes us to feel the hopes and fears, the joys and sufferings

---

[1] Note how the whole story of treachery, the deepest tragedy of the Ballad, is told in three words at the end of the eighth line.

of persons of all classes whether it be of the great and high-strung or of ordinary people in the common round of life, of the husbandman at the plough as much as the hero in the battle-field. There is moreover a strong and compelling charm in his language, which is partly due to the fact that no other poet's verse suits so perfectly the thoughts and emotions expressed. This is why his lines haunt us and are unforgettable. Tennyson used to say that Virgil's finest hexameters occur in the *Georgics* and in the sixth *Aeneid*. He has a wondrous diversity of cadences. He produces a remarkable effect by his variety in the use of the pause. Thus, in his description of a summer tempest in the *Georgics*, the varying breaks in the verse bring out the successive phases of the storm[1]. We may compare Milton's wonderful lines on his blindness, which close

> Thus with the year
> Seasons return, but not to me returns
> Day, or the sweet approach of ev'n or morn,
> Or sight of vernal bloom, or summer's rose,
> Or flocks, or herds, or human face divine[2].

Nothing could surpass the music of the latter passage. This is not mere metrical art. It is the great breath of inspiration behind the words which causes them to drop spontaneously into harmonious order.

Two well-known lines might also be instanced:

> Sed fugit interea, fugit irreparabile tempus,
> Singula dum capti circumvectamur amore[3].

The contrast between the swift flight of time and the fond lingering over things we delight in could not be better emphasized. Sometimes a single line gives Virgil scope for a metrical contrast as when he describes the

---

[1] *G.* I, 328–34. See notes.

[2] "Imagine this passage to be in prose 'Seasons return but not to me returns day' and we realize at once how much the 'natural pause' at the end of the line adds to the effect in verse." H. A. W.

[3] *G.* III, 284–5.

horse galloping now over broken ground and rocks, now in the level bed of deep valleys.

> Saxa per et scopulos et depressas convalles[1].

There are countless other instances such as the frogs croaking,

> Et veterem in limo ranae cecinere querelam[2],

or the ponderous seals lying down to sleep,

> Sternunt se somno diversae in litore phocae[3],

or the line enforcing the necessity of pains-taking where the ponderous closing word drives the lesson home.

> Scilicet omnibus est labor impendendus[4].

How are we to explain the extraordinary break after 'tanto' in the following line? Anyone familiar with Virgil must feel that it is there for a purpose.

> Nec rapit inmensos orbes per humum, neque tanto
> Squameus in spiram tractu se colligit anguis[5].

Is it not in order to compel us to stress 'tanto,' the huge spire of the serpent rising to strike? Virgil is claiming that Italy does not breed monstrous serpents as does the East. Notable also is the use of a marked pause after an opening spondee to emphasize the solemn or the supernatural.

> Vox quoque per lucos vulgo exaudita silentes
> Ingens, et simulacra modis pallentia miris
> Visa sub obscurum noctis[6].

---

[1] *G.* III, 276.
[2] *G.* I, 378, *c* of course pronounced *k*.
[3] *G.* IV, 432.
[4] *G.* II, 61. But when so fine a Virgilian scholar as Mr Page says that the superfluous syllable at the end of the line *G.* I, 295 'decoquit humor | em' suggests the boiling over of the pot, we feel that an accident is over-interpreted.
[5] *G.* II, 153–4.   [6] *G.* I, 476–8.

Virgil's metrical effects somehow do not impress us with the sense of artificiality as Tennyson's sometimes do, for example:

> Myriads of rivulets hurrying through the lawn,
> The moan of doves in immemorial elms,
> And murmuring of innumerable bees!

Here a sense of conscious intent interferes with the real beauty of the lines[1].

Lucretius' influence is felt everywhere in the *Georgics* but is specially prominent in the second where, as Munro has shown[2], his mind is completely "saturated" with the ideas and expressions of Lucretius. One of the most daring figures in the *De Rerum Natura* occurs where the poet is picturing how in the great burst of life on the new-born earth the first trees vied with each other as if running a race,

> arboribusque datumst variis exinde per auras
> crescendi magnum inmissis certamen habenis[3].

"Then there fell upon all kinds of trees a mighty rivalry of climbing up into the air like steeds racing at full gallop." To one watching the progress of different trees in spring, they do seem striving which shall outstrip the other. Virgil borrows this figure and applies it in weakened form to the young vine-shoot rejoicing in its power of growth[4]. If we wish to compare the two poets we might turn to Virgil's description of the ox whose companion,

---

[1] Mr H. A. Webster writes: "Is this criticism quite just? There may be a shadow of over-elaboration in the first line, but surely not in the last two. These are just the sounds which appeal to one in the fresh country, all of them perhaps in one moment of time and brought together by Nature herself. The myriads of rivulets hurrying have just a touch of the artificial which is emphasized by the use of the rather super-poetic word 'lawn.'"

[2] See his note on *G.* III, 449.

[3] v, 786. Baring's vigorous rendering is partly followed,

[4]   Dum se laetus ad auras
    Palmes agit, laxis per purum inmissus habenis.
                                           G. II, 363-4.

stricken by the plague, has dropped dead at the plough.
He refuses to work with a new yoke-fellow or to take food
and lows pitifully until he too dies. We might then turn
to Lucretius' wonderful picture of the cow whose calf has
been sacrificed[1], searching wood and meadow in vain,
desisting, and again and again returning to her stall and
then renewing her search, "nor can the soft willows and
grass quickened with dew and yon rivers gliding level
with their banks comfort her mind and put away the
care that has entered into her[2]." The influence of the
older poet on Virgil here is unmistakable. Lucretius
always sees Nature for himself, through his own eyes.
In this instance he still more than Virgil has sorrowed
with the poor four-footed creature and expressed the
actual verity of her passion. (And yet how fine and how
truly Virgilian is that detail! "What profit has the ox
of all the heavy clods he has turned up with the plough-
share?") Turning from Lucretius to Virgil is like coming
down from the keen air of the mountain-tops with their
Divine quiet and solitude to the lower ground where we
can scent the peat-smoke rising from the cottages and
hear the sounds of every-day life. Lucretius cannot help
being the more vivid of the two, but Virgil has struck
many a note of the human heart which the older poet
never touched.

Sainte-Beuve has said that every poem which is to
move and charm the readers of its day, "must, in some
way or other be grafted into its own period." The
remoteness of its subject even in the distant past need not
interfere with the interest but may even allow the poet's
imagination more scope, "But in some essential part of
the poem, through some main channel of its inspiration
it must possess present-day-ness, it must appropriate and
apply main events of the poet's own time. It must be
living for once at least, if it is to live for ever[3]." The

---

[1] Lucr. II, 349–66.
[2] Compare with this last touch G. III, 520–2.
[3] *Étude sur Virgile*, p. 82.

Georgics as we have seen fulfils this condition completely. The loss of the old Roman ideals and the degeneration of the Roman people, the crime of the rivals whose selfish ambition produced so many civil wars, the guilt of the nation and the anger of the Gods, the murder of a great leader who had brought hope to the world, the new hopes centred in the young Augustus—these things form the background of the *Georgics*. Virgil's world is all out of joint. How then does his poem stand related to it? In this way. Like Rousseau, but in an infinitely nobler sense, he holds that all such misery exists because men have departed from Nature and are living an insincere and artificial life. Ambition, greed and luxury have destroyed the fellow-feeling between man and man. It is not in the crowded cities where human beings degenerate in both soul and body, some drunken with the constant excitements of luxury, others degraded by extreme of poverty—it is not here that true pleasure is to be found. Virgil longs to recall men to the Simple Life and reminds them of its true and noble delights. The struggle with Nature's forces is necessary for man, it calls his manhood out. Husbandry may be a hard but yet is a just task-mistress: "Earth gives all their due," *iustissima Tellus*. Moreover the intimate contact with the sights and life of the country satisfies the sense of beauty which is an integral part of man, and also brings him into true and living touch with the great Spiritual power behind Nature. What Rome needs, the poet shows, is to be recalled to the elemental instincts of natural living which have been perverted within her, but may yet be restored. The farmer's existence has no luxuries or gorgeous surroundings, but "it brings repose without anxiety and a life where fraud and pretence are unknown."

At secura quies et nescia fallere vita.

Those who have studied the passages of the *Georgics* which are so full of Virgil's own personality know the actual world in which the poet lived: they know in how healthy a soil his youth was rooted, the great national crisis of Civil War which had caused such dangers and anxieties to the poet himself in his manhood but which brought him out of the world of art and exquisiteness into living touch with all the hopes and fears of human kind. During those troublous years his own ideals of living both as man and patriot had developed and grown clear and potent. These are largely expressed in one weighty word often recurring in the *Aeneid* but which never once meets us in the *Georgics*—that is *pietas*, the sense of duty and honour and of goodwill and mercy to man. But the *Georgics* too are deeply inspired by that sense. Doubtless Virgil required the many living figures of the *Aeneid* in order to express his own reading of the world and make us feel the pathos of human life as he, with years, increasingly felt it. The *Georgics* reveal to us the growth in mind and sympathies of the man whose great Epic was to become for all time, but especially to those dark Middle Ages when all other lights were obscured, a bright star of hope and guiding in the doubtful paths of life.

V. VIRGIL'S INFLUENCE ON THE EARLIEST BRITISH NATURE-POETRY

Gavin Douglas and Alexander Hume. Metrical improvements made by Douglas. His veneration for Virgil.

It is worth noting that the earliest Nature-poetry of Britain has been composed under the influence and inspiration of Virgil. We are often told that this influence was first manifested in Thomson's *Seasons*, a poem which few now read. Thus Stopford Brooke says that "the Naturalist poetry, both for human nature and Nature, began in modern English Literature with Thomson[1]." This does great injustice to a writer of higher and stronger gift. The Scottish Bishop, Gavin Douglas, in his version of the *Aeneid* produced the earliest translation of any Latin poet into verse in our country. The task occupied him for eighteen months and was completed on the feast of Mary Magdalen, a few weeks before two of his brothers fell at Flodden in the disastrous year 1513. Douglas was not merely a translator: he prefixes to every book of the *Aeneid* a verse Prologue. These Prologues not only express his admiration for Virgil and comment on the spirit and teaching of each book but two of them, the Seventh and the Twelfth, contain pictures one of mid-winter and the other of summer in the open country. What he has written in this vein, though so small in amount, is singularly sincere, truthfully painted and original. To borrow his own saying about Virgil, Douglas "has his eye directly upon the object" he describes[2]. He loves to depict the scenery of Scotland not merely in its cultivated districts, but rather in its wilder aspects of mountain and moor and river in spate, in winter storm rather than in summer and sunshine, a feature which is common to him with later

---

[1] *Naturalism in English Poetry*, Lecture I, 1910.
[2] In Prologue I he says of Virgil as a poet that his work is
Pleasable, perfect and feelable (intelligible) in all degree
As who the matter held before his ee.

Scottish poets. Virgil on the other hand delights rather in the beauty of mead and woodland and cultivated field.

Douglas greatly admires Chaucer, whose influence is very evident in his two longer poems, *King Hart* and *The Palace of Honour*. Contrasting himself with Chaucer, he says

> Far as he stands beneath Virgil in degree
> Under him as far I count myself to be,

a modest estimate, for he holds the gulf between those two poets to be wide indeed. Chaucer is fond of using the conventional May-time introduction, which had become the fashion in poetry since the *Romance of the Rose*. He loves to begin with the sweet singing of the birds, the flowers opening in the green meads, the genial air of spring, all painted with his exquisite simplicity and charm. But Douglas does not, like him, confine himself to a few, almost stereotyped, cheerful features of the spring. He goes far beyond Chaucer in his intimate observation of every sign of the season in earth and sky. Thus he writes, with an artist's keen appreciation of the ferns and weeds reddened by the winter cold,

> The wind made wave the red weed on the dyke,

and when summer has returned, he rejoices to see how

> The rosé knoppís (rose-buds) pushing forth their head
> Gan chip (burst) and show their vermel (vermilion) lippís red.

Such touches of delight in beauty and colour are far more akin to Burns and even to Keats than to the poet of the *Seasons* with his vague renderings of natural objects. But of the enjoyment of beauty is born the striving to catch and faithfully express "with the eye direct upon it" the distinctive feature of each object. This ranks Douglas with the great poets of the nineteenth century. Out of this attitude is developed in course of time what Matthew Arnold has called "natural magic": to Keats or Wordsworth the thing seen by the eye reveals many things which are not seen. The nightingale or the daffodils dancing in the breeze have power to give form to our inner thoughts and to suggest images that flash light on all the mysteries of our life.

In the Seventh Prologue which follows the marvellous vision of Heaven and Hell in Book VI he gives a picture of a mid-winter day in Scotland, savage with snow and sleet and dark-shadowed skies from which at times lightning breaks. The gloom and naked trees and fields suggest to him

> Ghostly shadows of age and grisly death.

The poem is saturated with the very smell of snow in the air. Douglas seems to revel in the fierceness of the storm which makes animals' hair to 'grue' (shudder) and compels all, both tame and wild, to seek shelter—

> The small birds, flocking through thick brambles thrang (thronged)
> In chirming (plaintive cries) and with cheeping changed their song[1],
> Seeking for nooks and corners them to hide
> From fearful thuds (blasts) of the tempestuous tide (weather).

Along with Douglas another Scottish poet deserves to be named, Alexander Hume, one of a distinguished Border family who took their stand with Knox and the Protestant nobles at the Reformation time. After practising for some years as an advocate Hume became a Churchman and in 1599 published a small volume of verse. This contains a remarkable poem of over 200 lines called *The Day Estivall*, a description of a perfect summer day. Man's rejoicing in the warmth and fresh wholesomeness and rich beauty of summer has never been more sincerely expressed. Hume has not merely an intense love of nature but also the artist's keen eye for those details which signify.

> The misty rocke, the clouds of rain   haze
> From tops of mountains skails;   scatters
> Clear are the highest hills and plains;
> The vapour takes the vales.

[1] Notes of alarm alternated with their ordinary ones.

Begaried is the sapphire pend   The sapphire vault is variegated
With spraings of scarlet hue,   streaks
And preciously from end to end   exquisitely
Damasked white and blue.   patterned in

The ample heaven of fabric sure
In cleanness does surpass
The crystal and the silver pure,
Or clearest polished glass.

The time so tranquil is and still
That nowhere shall ye find,
Save on ane high and barren hill,
An air of peeping wind.   A breath of whispering wind

All trees and simples great and small,   herbs
That balmy leaf do bear,
Nor they were painted on a wall,
No more they move or stir.

Calm is the deep and purple sea,
Yet smoother nor the sand;
The walls that weltering wont to be   waves
Are stable like the land[1].

Hume's poems show that he knows Virgil well, though he has not assimilated Virgil's thought and ideals as Douglas has. Both Douglas and Hume stand directly in the line of poetic development between Virgil and the great nature-poetry of the nineteenth century; they bear no trace of the somewhat artificial tone which marks Thomson's *Seasons*.

Not only has Douglas' love of the Roman poet lent dignity to his style, but it was certainly through his close and life-long study of Virgil that he acquired also a mastery of verse which, in certain respects, no other English poet had up to his day attained and this in spite of his very archaic dialect. Courthope has summed up these metrical improvements in his *History of English Poetry*[2]. He contrasts "the noble and beautiful versifica-

[1] From Professor Lawson's excellent edition of Hume (Scottish Text Society), 1902. In this passage and in the extracts from Douglas I have modernised the spelling.

[2] Vol. 1, p. 379.

tion of Douglas" with the almost total lack of metrical harmony in the English contemporary poets. Compared with these "the rhythmical movement of Douglas' stanzas in *King Hart* is the very soul of melody." His verse also gained swiftness of movement as compared even with Chaucer from his "protraction of the sentence," which is linked together by subordinate clauses as in Latin, and thus takes the place of several short sentences, often of a single line, seldom extending beyond two lines. Courthope also notes "true pathos and nobility" in the style of his translation.

When we study the other Prologues we see that the great Humanist and the Scottish poet are deeply in accord. The things which both hold most precious are the same. They are profoundly akin to each other in ethical temper and in depth of religious sense. No poet, not even Dante, has been more truly inspired by Virgil than has Douglas. In order to express his heart-felt reverence for his Master, he has sought an image derived from the public worship of Christendom, that most sacred moment of the Mass when, at the tinkle of the bell, the priest raised up the Host before it was transformed into the actual body of God and all the worshippers fell on their knees.

Master of masters, sweet source and springing well.
Wide where o'er all ringís thy heavenly bell;
I mean thy crafty workís curious[1],
So quick, lusty and most sententious[2]...
Why should I then with dull forhede and wane[3],
With rude engíne (faculty) and barren empty brain,
With bad harsh speech and lewit (ignorant), barbour tongue,
Presume to write where thy sweet bell is rung
Or counterfeit so precious wordís dear?
No, no, not so but kneel when I them hear.

[1] Skilful and exquisite writings.
[2] So vivid, pleasant and full of wisdom.
[3] With dull and futile wit.

GEORGICS

BOOK I

Ll. **1-5**. Subject of the Poem. **71-83**. Alternate farming. After a harvest of grain either let the land lie fallow or change the crop. **118-146**. The blessing and dignity of Labour. Jupiter has ordained the husband-man's life to be hard out of kindness to man that he may develop character and invention. **147-168**. If the farmer does not combat weeds and briars, his crops fail. **193-203**. The tendency of things to degenerate. But steady industry can combat this. **259-275**. Work for bad weather and holidays. **287-310**. Winter the season for festivities and sport. **316-335**. Storm in full Summer. **351-382**. Weather-signs ordained by Jupiter that the farmer may not be taken unawares. **393-423**. Signs of Rain. **461-497**. Sympathy of Nature with man: portents before and after Caesar's murder. **498-514**. From East to West Rome's enemies threaten. May the young Augustus be spared to save his country!

1-5. *Subject of the Poem.*

Quid faciat laetas segetes, quo sidere terram
vertere, Maecenas, ulmisque adiungere vites
conveniat: quae cura boum, qui cultus habendo
sit pecori; apibus quanta experientia parcis;
hinc canere incipiam.   5

71-83. *Alternate farming. After a harvest of grain either let the land lie fallow or change the crop.*

Alternis idem tonsas cessare novales,
et segnem patiere situ durescere campum;
aut ibi flava seres mutato sidere farra,
unde prius laetum siliqua quassante legumen
aut tenuis fetus viciae tristisque lupini   75
sustuleris fragiles calamos silvamque sonantem.

urit enim lini campum seges, urit avenae,
urunt Lethaeo perfusa papavera somno.
sed tamen alternis facilis labor, arida tantum
ne saturare fimo pingui pudeat sola neve   80
effetos cinerem inmundum iactare per agros.
sic quoque mutatis requiescunt fetibus arva;
nec nulla interea est inaratae gratia terrae.

118–146. *The blessing and dignity of Labour. Jupiter
has ordained the husbandman's life to be hard out of kindness to man that he may develop character and invention.*

Nec tamen, haec cum sint hominumque boumque
      labores
versando terram experti, nihil improbus anser
Strymoniaeque grues et amaris intuba fibris   120
officiunt aut umbra nocet. Pater ipse colendi
haud facilem esse viam voluit, primusque per artem
movit agros curis acuens mortalia corda,
nec torpere gravi passus sua regna veterno.
ante Iovem nulli subigebant arva coloni;   125
ne signare quidem aut partiri limite campum
fas erat: in medium quaerebant, ipsaque tellus
omnia liberius nullo poscente ferebat.
ille malum virus serpentibus addidit atris,
praedarique lupos iussit pontumque moveri,   130
mellaque decussit foliis, ignemque removit,
et passim rivis currentia vina repressit,
ut varias usus meditando extunderet artes
paulatim, et sulcis frumenti quaereret herbam,
ut silicis venis abstrusum excuderet ignem.   135
tunc alnos primum fluvii sensere cavatas;
navita tum stellis numeros et nomina fecit
Pleiadas, Hyadas, claramque Lycaonis Arcton;
tum laqueis captare feras et fallere visco
inventum, et magnos canibus circumdare saltus;   140
atque alius latum funda iam verberat amnem,

alta petens pelagoque alius trahit umida lina;
tum ferri rigor atque argutae lamina serrae,
—nam primi cuneis scindebant fissile lignum—
tum variae venere artes. labor omnia vicit   145
improbus et duris urgens in rebus egestas.

   147–168. If the farmer does not combat weeds and
                briars, his crops fail.

Prima Ceres ferro mortales vertere terram
instituit, cum iam glandes atque arbuta sacrae
deficerent silvae, et victum Dodona negaret.
mox et frumentis labor additus, ut mala culmos   150
esset robigo, segnisque horreret in arvis
carduus: intereunt segetes, subit aspera silva,
lappaeque tribulique, interque nitentia culta
infelix lolium et steriles dominantur avenae.
quod nisi et assiduis herbam insectabere rastris,   155
et sonitu terrebis aves, et ruris opaci
falce premes umbras, votisque vocaveris imbrem;
heu! magnum alterius frustra spectabis acervum,
concussaque famem in silvis solabere quercu.
dicendum et, quae sint duris agrestibus arma,   160
quis sine nec potuere seri nec surgere messes:
vomis et inflexi primum grave robur aratri,
tardaque Eleusinae matris volventia plaustra,
tribulaque traheaeque et iniquo pondere rastri;
virgea praeterea Celeï vilisque supellex,   165
arbuteae crates et mystica vannus Iacchi:
omnia quae multo ante memor provisa repones,
si te digna manet divini gloria ruris.

   193–203. The tendency of things to degenerate.

Semina vidi equidem multos medicare serentes,
et nitro prius et nigra perfundere amurga,
grandior ut fetus siliquis fallacibus esset,   195
et, quamvis igni exiguo, properata maderent.
vidi lecta diu et multo spectata labore

degenerare tamen, ni vis humana quotannis
maxima quaeque manu legeret. sic omnia fatis
in peius ruere ac retro sublapsa referri,   200
non aliter quam qui adverso vix flumine lembum
remigiis subigit, si bracchia forte remisit,
atque illum in praeceps prono rapit alveus amni.

259–275. *Work for bad weather and holidays.*

Frigidus agricolam si quando continet imber,
multa, forent quae mox caelo properanda sereno,
maturare datur: durum procudit arator   261
vomeris obtunsi dentem, cavat arbore lintres,
aut pecori signum aut numeros inpressit acervis.
exacuunt alii vallos furcasque bicornes,
atque Amerina parant lentae retinacula viti.   265
nunc facilis rubea texatur fiscina virga,
nunc torrete igni fruges, nunc frangite saxo.
quippe etiam festis quaedam exercere diebus
fas et iura sinunt: rivos deducere nulla
religio vetuit, segeti praetendere saepem,   270
insidias avibus moliri, incendere vepres,
balantumque gregem fluvio mersare salubri.
saepe oleo tardi costas agitator aselli
vilibus aut onerat pomis, lapidemque revertens
incusum aut atrae massam picis urbe reportat.   275

287–310. *Winter the season for festivities and sport.*

Multa adeo gelida melius se nocte dedere,
aut cum sole novo terras irrorat Eous.
nocte leves melius stipulae, nocte arida prata
tondentur; noctes lentus non deficit humor.   290
et quidam seros hiberni ad luminis ignes
pervigilat, ferroque faces inspicat acuto;
interea longum cantu solata laborem
arguto coniux percurrit pectine telas;
aut dulcis musti Vulcano decoquit humorem   295
et foliis undam trepidi despumat aheni.

at rubicunda Ceres medio succiditur aestu;
et medio tostas aestu terit area fruges.
nudus ara, sere nudus; hiems ignava colono.
frigoribus parto agricolae plerumque fruuntur,   300
mutuaque inter se laeti convivia curant.
invitat genialis hiems curasque resolvit:
ceu pressae cum iam portum tetigere carinae,
puppibus et laeti nautae imposuere coronas.
sed tamen et quernas glandes tum stringere tempus,
et lauri bacas, oleamque, cruentaque myrta;   306
tum gruibus pedicas et retia ponere cervis,
auritosque sequi lepores; tum figere dammas,
stuppea torquentem Balearis verbera fundae: 309
cum nix alta iacet, glaciem cum flumina trudunt.

316–335. *Storm in full Summer.*

Saepe ego, cum flavis messorem induceret arvis
agricola et fragili iam stringeret hordea culmo,
omnia ventorum concurrere proelia vidi,
quae gravidam late segetem ab radicibus imis
sublimem expulsam eruerent, ita turbine nigro   320
ferret hiems culmumque levem stipulasque volantes.
saepe etiam inmensum caelo venit agmen aquarum,
et foedam glomerant tempestatem imbribus atris
collectae ex alto nubes; ruit arduus aether,
et pluvia ingenti sata laeta boumque labores   325
diluit; inplentur fossae et cava flumina crescunt
cum sonitu fervetque fretis spirantibus aequor.
ipse Pater media nimborum in nocte corusca
fulmina molitur dextra: quo maxima motu
terra tremit; fugere ferae et mortalia corda   330
per gentes humilis stravit pavor: ille flagranti
aut Athon aut Rhodopen aut alta Ceraunia telo
deiicit; ingeminant Austri et densissimus imber:
nunc nemora ingenti vento, nunc litora plangunt.
hoc metuens caeli menses et sidera serva.   335

351-382. *Weather-signs ordained by Jupiter that
the farmer may not be taken unawares.*

Atque haec ut certis possimus discere signis,
aestusque, pluviasque, et agentes frigora ventos,
ipse Pater statuit, quid menstrua Luna moneret,
quo signo caderent Austri; quid saepe videntes
agricolae propius stabulis armenta tenerent.   355
continuo, ventis surgentibus, aut freta ponti
incipiunt agitata tumescere, et aridus altis
montibus audiri fragor, aut resonantia longe
litora misceri, et nemorum increbrescere murmur.
iam sibi tum curvis male temperat unda carinis,   360
cum medio celeres revolant ex aequore mergi,
clamoremque ferunt ad litora, cumque marinae
in sicco ludunt fulicae, notasque paludes
deserit, atque altam supra volat ardea nubem.
saepe etiam stellas vento impendente videbis   365
praecipites caelo labi, noctisque per umbram
flammarum longos a tergo albescere tractus;
saepe levem paleam et frondes volitare caducas,
aut summa nantes in aqua colludere plumas.
at Boreae de parte trucis cum fulminat, et cum   370
Eurique Zephyrique tonat domus, omnia plenis
rura natant fossis, atque omnis navita ponto
humida vela legit. numquam imprudentibus imber
obfuit: aut illum surgentem vallibus imis
aëriae fugere grues, aut bucula caelum   375
suspiciens patulis captavit naribus auras,
aut arguta lacus circumvolitavit hirundo
et veterem in limo ranae cecinere querelam.
saepius et tectis penetralibus extulit ova
angustum formica terens iter, et bibit ingens   380
arcus, et e pastu decedens agmine magno
corvorum increpuit densis exercitus alis.

393–423. *Signs of Rain.*

Nec minus ex imbri soles et aperta serena
prospicere et certis poteris cognoscere signis:
nam neque tum stellis acies obtusa videtur,   395
nec fratris radiis obnoxia surgere Luna,
tenuia nec lanae per caelum vellera ferri;
non tepidum ad solem pennas in litore pandunt
dilectae Thetidi alcyones; non ore solutos
immundi meminere sues iactare maniplos: 400
at nebulae magis ima petunt campoque recumbunt;
solis et occasum servans de culmine summo
nequidquam seros exercet noctua cantus.
apparet liquido sublimis in aëre Nisus,
et pro purpureo poenas dat Scylla capillo.   405
quacumque illa levem fugiens secat aethera pennis,
ecce inimicus, atrox, magno stridore per auras
insequitur Nisus: qua se fert Nisus ad auras,
illa levem fugiens raptim secat aethera pennis.
tum liquidas corvi presso ter gutture voces   410
aut quater ingeminant; et saepe cubilibus altis,
nescio qua praeter solitum dulcedine laeti,
inter se in foliis strepitant; iuvat imbribus actis
progeniem parvam dulcesque revisere nidos:
haud, equidem credo, quia sit divinitus illis   415
ingenium, aut rerum fato prudentia maior:
verum, ubi tempestas et caeli mobilis humor
mutavere vias, et Iupiter uvidus Austris
denset, erant quae rara modo, et, quae densa, relaxat;
vertuntur species animorum, et pectora motus   420
nunc alios, alios, dum nubila ventus agebat,
concipiunt. hinc ille avium concentus in agris,
et laetae pecudes, et ovantes gutture corvi.

*461–497. Sympathy of Nature with man:
Portents during the year of Caesar's murder.*

Denique, quid vesper serus vehat, unde serenas
ventus agat nubes, quid cogitet humidus Auster,
sol tibi signa dabit. solem quis dicere falsum
audeat? ille etiam caecos instare tumultus
saepe monet, fraudemque et operta tumescere bella.
ille etiam exstincto miseratus Caesare Romam: 466
cum caput obscura nitidum ferrugine texit,
impiaque aeternam timuerunt saecula noctem.
tempore quamquam illo tellus quoque, et aequora
    ponti,
obscenaeque canes, importunaeque volucres   470
signa dabant. quoties Cyclopum effervere in agros
vidimus undantem ruptis fornacibus Aetnam,
flammarumque globos liquefactaque volvere saxa!
armorum sonitum toto Germania caelo
audiit, insolitis tremuerunt motibus Alpes.   475
vox quoque per lucos vulgo exaudita silentes
ingens, et simulacra modis pallentia miris
visa sub obscurum noctis, pecudesque locutae,
infandum! sistunt amnes terraeque dehiscunt,
et maestum inlacrimat templis ebur aeraque sudant.
proluit insano contorquens vertice silvas   481
fluviorum rex Eridanus, camposque per omnes
cum stabulis armenta tulit. nec tempore eodem
tristibus aut extis fibrae apparere minaces
aut puteis manare cruor cessavit, et altae   485
per noctem resonare lupis ululantibus urbes.
non alias caelo ceciderunt plura sereno
fulgura, nec diri totiens arsere cometae.
ergo inter sese paribus concurrere telis
Romanas acies iterum videre Philippi;   490
nec fuit indignum superis, bis sanguine nostro
Emathiam et latos Haemi pinguescere campos.

scilicet et tempus veniet, cum finibus illis
agricola incurvo terram molitus aratro
exesa inveniet scabra robigine pila,   495
aut gravibus rastris galeas pulsabit inanes,
grandiaque effossis mirabitur ossa sepulchris.

498–514. *From East to West Rome's enemies threaten.*
May the young Augustus be spared to save his country!

Di patrii, Indigetes, et Romule Vestaque mater,
quae Tuscum Tiberim et Romana Palatia servas,
hunc saltem everso iuvenem succurrere saeclo   500
ne prohibete. satis iam pridem sanguine nostro
Laomedonteae luimus periuria Troiae,
iam pridem nobis caeli te regia, Caesar,
invidet, atque hominum queritur curare triumphos,
quippe ubi fas versum atque nefas; tot bella per
    orbem,   505
tam multae scelerum facies; non ullus aratro
dignus honos; squalent abductis arva colonis,
et curvae rigidum falces conflantur in ensem.
hinc movet Euphrates, illinc Germania bellum;
vicinae ruptis inter se legibus urbes   510
arma ferunt; saevit toto Mars impius orbe:
ut cum carceribus sese effudere quadrigae,
addunt in spatia, et frustra retinacula tendens
fertur equis auriga, neque audit currus habenas.

BOOK II

Ll. **1–8**. A new subject. Father Bacchus is invoked. **35–82**. How to grow Vine and Olive. Fruit-trees cannot be left to Nature; the art of grafting. **109–122, 136–176**. Glory of Italy. Hail to the Saturnian land, mother of noble fruits and a heroic breed of men! **315–345**. Spring-time, the birth-day of the world. **362–370**. The young vine is sensitive and shrinks from the knife. **458–474**. Happiness of the husbandman. **475–494**. Virgil reveres Lucretius for his insight into Nature and her Laws. But the rivers and the woods which he loves are *his* teachers and also the Gods of the country. **495–542**. Calm and happiness of the country compared with the ambition and greed of city-life. The countryman rejoices in the work of his hands. It was in such clean and strenuous living that Rome waxed strong and became the glory of the earth.

1–8. *A new subject. Father Bacchus is invoked.*

Hactenus arvorum cultus et sidera caeli,
nunc te, Bacche, canam, nec non silvestria tecum
virgulta et prolem tarde crescentis olivae.
huc, pater o Lenaee; tuis hic omnia plena
muneribus, tibi pampineo gravidus autumno   5
floret ager, spumat plenis vindemia labris;
huc, pater o Lenaee, veni, nudataque musto
tingue novo mecum dereptis crura cothurnis.

35–82. *How to grow Vine and Olive. Fruit-trees cannot be left to Nature: the art of grafting.*

Quare agite o, proprios generatim discite cultus,   35
agricolae, fructusque feros mollite colendo;
neu segnes iaceant terrae. iuvat Ismara Baccho
conserere, atque olea magnum vestire Taburnum.
tuque ades, inceptumque una decurre laborem,

o decus, o famae merito pars maxima nostrae, 40
Maecenas, pelagoque volans da vela patenti.
non ego cuncta meis amplecti versibus opto;
non, mihi si linguae centum sint, oraque centum,
ferrea vox: ades, et primi lege litoris oram.
in manibus terrae: non hic te carmine ficto 45
atque per ambages et longa exorsa tenebo.
sponte sua quae se tollunt in luminis oras,
infecunda quidem, sed laeta et fortia surgunt;
quippe solo natura subest. tamen haec quoque si quis
inserat, aut scrobibus mandet mutata subactis, 50
exuerint silvestrem animum; cultuque frequenti
in quascumque voces artes haud tarda sequentur.
nec non et sterilis, quae stirpibus exit ab imis,
hoc faciet, vacuos si sit digesta per agros:
nunc altae frondes et rami matris opacant, 55
crescentique adimunt fetus, uruntque ferentem.
iam, quae seminibus iactis se sustulit arbos,
tarda venit, seris factura nepotibus umbram;
pomaque degenerant sucos oblita priores;
et turpes avibus praedam fert uva racemos. 60
scilicet omnibus est labor impendendus, et omnes
cogendae in sulcum, ac multa mercede domandae.
sed truncis oleae melius, propagine vites
respondent, solido Paphiae de robore myrtus;
plantis et durae coruli nascuntur, et ingens 65
fraxinus, Herculeaeque arbos umbrosa coronae,
Chaoniique patris glandes; etiam ardua palma
nascitur, et casus abies visura marinos.
inseritur vero et fetu nucis arbutus horrida,
et steriles platani malos gessere valentes; 70
castaneae fagus, ornusque incanuit albo
flore piri, glandemque sues fregere sub ulmis.
nec modus inserere atque oculos imponere simplex.
nam, qua se medio trudunt de cortice gemmae,
et tenues rumpunt tunicas, angustus in ipso 75

fit nodo sinus: huc aliena ex arbore germen
includunt, udoque docent inolescere libro.
aut rursum enodes trunci resecantur, et alte
finditur in solidum cuneis via; deinde feraces
plantae immittuntur: nec longum tempus, et ingens
exiit ad coelum ramis felicibus arbos,   81
miraturque novas frondes et non sua poma.

109–122, 136–176. *Glory of Italy, Hail to the Saturnian
   land, mother of noble fruits and a heroic breed of men!*

Nec vero terrae ferre omnes omnia possunt.
fluminibus salices crassisque paludibus alni   110
nascuntur, steriles saxosis montibus orni:
litora myrtetis laetissima; denique apertos
Bacchus amat collis, aquilonem et frigora taxi.
aspice et extremis domitum cultoribus orbem,
Eoasque domos Arabum pictosque Gelonos: 115
divisae arboribus patriae. sola India nigrum
fert ebenum, solis est turea virga Sabaeis.
quid tibi odorato referam sudantia ligno
balsamaque et bacas semper frondentis acanthi?
quid nemora Aethiopum, molli canentia lana?   120
velleraque ut foliis depectant tenuia Seres?
aut quos Oceano propior gerit India lucos,...
sed neque Medorum, silvae ditissima, terra
nec pulcher Ganges atque auro turbidus Hermus
laudibus Italiae certent, non Bactra, neque Indi,
totaque turiferis Panchaia pinguis arenis.
haec loca non tauri spirantes naribus ignem   140
invertere satis immanis dentibus hydri,
nec galeis densisque virum seges horruit hastis;
sed gravidae fruges et Bacchi Massicus humor
implevere; tenent oleae armentaque laeta.
hinc bellator equus campo sese arduus infert;   145
hinc albi, Clitumne, greges et maxima taurus
victima, saepe tuo perfusi flumine sacro,

Romanos ad templa deum duxere triumphos.
hic ver adsiduum atque alienis mensibus aestas;
bis gravidae pecudes, bis pomis utilis arbos.   150
at rabidae tigres absunt et saeva leonum
semina, nec miseros fallunt aconita legentes,
nec rapit immensos orbes per humum, neque tanto
squameus in spiram tractu se colligit anguis.
adde tot egregias urbes operumque laborem,   155
tot congesta manu praeruptis oppida saxis,
fluminaque antiquos subterlabentia muros.
an mare, quod supra, memorem, quodque adluit
     infra?
anne lacus tantos, te, Lari maxime, teque,
fluctibus et fremitu adsurgens Benace marino?   160
an memorem portus Lucrinoque addita claustra
atque indignatum magnis stridoribus aequor,
Iulia qua ponto longe sonat unda refuso
Tyrrhenusque fretis inmittitur aestus Avernis?
haec eadem argenti rivos aerisque metalla   165
ostendit venis, atque auro plurima fluxit.
haec genus acre virum, Marsos, pubemque Sabellam,
adsuetumque malo Ligurem, Volscosque verutos
extulit, haec Decios, Marios, magnosque Camillos,
Scipiadas duros bello, et te, maxume Caesar,   170
qui nunc extremis Asiae iam victor in oris
imbellem avertis Romanis arcibus Indum.
salve, magna parens frugum, Saturnia tellus,
magna virum; tibi res antiquae laudis et artis
ingredior, sanctos ausus recludere fontis,   175
Ascraeumque cano Romana per oppida carmen.

315–345. *Spring-time the birth-day of the world.*

Nec tibi tam prudens quisquam persuadeat auctor
tellurem Borea rigidam spirante movere.
rura gelu tunc claudit hiems, nec semine iacto
concretam patitur radicem adfigere terrae.

optima vinetis satio, cum vere rubenti
candida venit avis longis invisa colubris,   320
prima vel autumni sub frigora, cum rapidus Sol
nondum hiemem contingit equis, iam praeterit aestas.
ver adeo frondi nemorum, ver utile silvis,
vere tument terrae et genitalia semina poscunt.
tum pater omnipotens fecundis imbribus Aether   325
coniugis in gremium laetae descendit, et omnes
magnus alit, magno commixtus corpore, fetus.
avia tum resonant avibus virgulta canoris,
et Venerem certis repetunt armenta diebus;
parturit almus ager, Zephyrique tepentibus auris 330
laxant arva sinus; superat tener omnibus humor;
inque novos soles audent se germina tuto
credere; nec metuit surgentis pampinus austros
aut actum caelo magnis aquilonibus imbrem,
sed trudit gemmas et frondes explicat omnes.   335
non alios prima crescentis origine mundi
inluxisse dies aliumve habuisse tenorem
crediderim: ver illud erat, ver magnus agebat
orbis, et hibernis parcebant flatibus Euri:
cum primae lucem pecudes hausere, virumque   340
ferrea progenies duris caput extulit arvis,
immissaeque ferae silvis et sidera caelo.
nec res hunc tenerae possent perferre laborem,
si non tanta quies iret frigusque caloremque
inter, et exciperet caeli indulgentia terras.   345

362–370. *The young vine is sensitive and shrinks from the knife.*

Ac dum prima novis adolescit frondibus aetas,
parcendum teneris, et, dum se laetus ad auras
palmes agit laxis per purum immissus habenis,
ipsa acie nondum falcis temptanda, sed uncis   365
carpendae manibus frondes, interque legendae:
inde ubi iam validis amplexae stirpibus ulmos

exierint, tunc stringe comas, tūnc bracchia tonde;
ante reformidant ferrum; tum denique dura
exerce imperia, et ramos compesce fluentes.   370

458–474. *Happiness of the husbandman.*

O fortunatos nimium, sua si bona norint,
agricolas, quibus ipsa, procul discordibus armis,
fundit humo facilem victum iustissima tellus!   460
si non ingentem foribus domus alta superbis
mane salutantum totis vomit aedibus undam,
nec varios inhiant pulchra testudine postes,
illusasque auro vestes, Ephyreiaque aera,
alba neque Assyrio fucatur lana veneno,   465
nec casia liquidi corrumpitur usus olivi:
at secura quies et nescia fallere vita,
dives opum variarum, at latis otia fundis,
speluncae, vivique lacus, at frigida Tempe,
mugitusque boum, mollesque sub arbore somni   470
non absunt; illic saltus ac lustra ferarum,
et patiens operum exiguoque adsueta iuventus,
sacra deum, sanctique patres; extrema per illos
Iustitia excedens terris vestigia fecit.

475–494. *Virgil reveres Lucretius for his insight into Nature and her Laws. But the rivers and the woods which he loves are his teachers and also the Gods of the country.*

Me vero primum dulces ante omnia Musae,   475
quarum sacra fero ingenti percussus amore,
accipiant, caelique vias et sidera monstrent;
defectus solis varios, lunaeque labores;
unde tremor terris; qua vi maria alta tumescant,
obicibus ruptis, rursusque in se ipsa residant;   480
quid tantum oceano properent se tingere soles
hiberni, vel quae tardis mora noctibus obstet.
sin, has ne possim naturae accedere partes,

frigidus obstiterit circum praecordia sanguis:
rura mihi et rigui placeant in vallibus amnes;   485
flumina amem silvasque inglorius. o, ubi campi
Spercheosque, et virginibus bacchata Lacaenis
Taügeta! o, qui me gelidis in vallibus Haemi
sistat, et ingenti ramorum protegat umbra!
felix, qui potuit rerum cognoscere causas,   490
atque metus omnes et inexorabile fatum
subiecit pedibus strepitumque Acherontis avari!
fortunatus et ille, deos qui novit agrestes
Panaque Silvanumque senem Nymphasque sorores!

*495–542. Calm and happiness of the country compared
with the ambition and greed of city-life. The countryman rejoices in the work of his hands. It was in such
clean and strenuous living that Rome waxed strong and
became the glory of the earth.*

Illum non populi fasces, non purpura regum   495
flexit et infidos agitans discordia fratres,
aut coniurato descendens Dacus ab Histro,
non res Romanae peritüraque regna; neque ille
aut doluit miserans inopem, aut invidit habenti.
quos rami fructus, quos ipsa volentia rura   500
sponte tulere sua, carpsit, nec ferrea iura
insanumque forum aut populi tabularia vidit.
sollicitant alii remis freta caeca, ruuntque
in ferrum, penetrant aulas et limina regum;
hic petit exscidiis urbem miserosque Penates,   505
ut gemma bibat et Sarrano dormiat ostro;
condit opes alius, defossoque incubat auro;
hic stupet attonitus rostris; hunc plausus hiantem
per cuneos geminatus enim plebisque patrumque
corripuit; gaudent perfusi sanguine fratrum,   510
exsilioque domos et dulcia limina mutant,
atque alio patriam quaerunt sub sole iacentem.
agricola incurvo terram dimovit aratro:

hinc anni labor, hinc patriam parvosque nepotes
sustinet, hinc armenta boum meritosque iuvencos.
nec requies, quin aut pomis exuberet annus,   516
aut fetu pecorum, aut Cerealis mergite culmi,
proventuque oneret sulcos atque horrea vincat.
venit hiems, teritur Sicyonia baca trapetis,
glande sues laeti redeunt, dant arbuta silvae;   520
et varios ponit fetus autumnus, et alte
mitis in apricis coquitur vindemia saxis.
interea dulces pendent circum oscula nati,
casta pudicitiam servat domus, ubera vaccae
lactea demittunt, pinguesque in gramine laeto   525
inter se adversis luctantur cornibus haedi.
ipse dies agitat festos, fususque per herbam,
ignis ubi in medio et socii cratera coronant,
te, libans, Lenaee, vocat, pecorisque magistris
velocis iaculi certamina ponit in ulmo,   530
corporaque agresti nudant praedura palaestrae.
hanc olim veteres vitam coluere Sabini,
hanc Remus et frater, sic fortis Etruria crevit
scilicet et rerum facta est pulcherrima Roma,
septemque una sibi muro circumdedit arces.   535
ante etiam sceptrum Dictaei regis, et ante
impia quam caesis gens est epulata iuvencis,
aureus hanc vitam in terris Saturnus agebat.
necdum etiam audierant inflari classica, necdum
impositos duris crepitare incudibus enses.   540
sed nos immensum spatiis confecimus aequor,
et iam tempus equum fumantia solvere colla.

BOOK III

Ll. 1–16, 26–33 ff. Rome must have a poetry of her own, not re-telling the old and outworn legends of Greece. I will bring the Muses to Italy and rear a temple to Caesar with his victories sculptured on the gates. 72–94. The points of a horse. 284–293. Virgil must hasten on to treat of sheep and goats—a humble subject for poetry but its novelty will carry him on. 515–530. Pestilence among cattle. The ox sorrowing for his yoke-fellow, fallen dead at the plough.

1–16, 26–33 ff. *Rome must have a poetry of her own, not re-telling the old and outworn legends of Greece. I will bring the Muses to Italy and rear a temple to Caesar with his victories sculptured on the gates.*

Te quoque, magna Pales, et te memorande canemus
pastor ab Amphryso; vos, silvae amnesque Lycaei.
cetera, quae vacuas tenuissent carmine mentes,
omnia iam vulgata. quis aut Eurysthea durum,
aut illaudati nescit Busiridis aras?   5
cui non dictus Hylas puer, et Latonia Delos,
Hippodameque, humeroque Pelops insignis eburno,
acer equis? temptanda via est, qua me quoque possim
tollere humo, victorque virum volitare per ora.
primus ego in patriam mecum, modo vita supersit,   10
Aonio rediens deducam vertice Musas;
primus Idumaeas referam tibi, Mantua, palmas;
et viridi in campo templum de marmore ponam
propter aquam, tardis ingens ubi flexibus errat
Mincius et tenera praetexit arundine ripas.   15
in medio mihi Caesar erit, templumque tenebit....
in foribus pugnam ex auro solidoque elephanto
Gangaridum faciam, victorisque arma Quirini;
atque hic undantem bello magnumque fluentem

Nilum, ac navali surgentes aere columnas.
addam urbes Asiae domitas pulsumque Niphaten,   30
fidentemque fuga Parthum versisque sagittis,
et duo rapta manu diverso ex hoste tropaea,
bisque triumphatas utroque ab litore gentes....
interea Dryadum silvas saltusque sequamur   40
intactos, tua, Maecenas, haud mollia iussa.
te sine nil altum mens incohat...
mox tamen ardentes accingar dicere pugnas   46
Caesaris et nomen fama tot ferre per annos
Tithoni prima quot abest ab origine Caesar.

72-94. *The points of a horse.*

Nec non et pecori est idem dilectus equino.
tu modo, quos in spem statues submittere gentis,
praecipuum iam inde a teneris impende laborem.
continuo pecoris generosi pullus in arvis   75
altius ingreditur, et mollia crura reponit.
primus et ire viam, et fluvios temptare minaces,
audet, et ignoto sese committere ponti;
nec vanos horret strepitus. illi ardua cervix,
argutumque caput, brevis alvus, obesaque terga; 80
luxuriatque toris animosum pectus. honesti
spadices, glaucique: color deterrimus albis,
et gilvo. tum, si qua sonum procul arma dedere,
stare loco nescit; micat auribus et tremit artus;
collectumque fremens volvit sub naribus ignem: 85
densa iuba, et dextro iactata recumbit in armo.
at duplex agitur per lumbos spina; cavatque
tellurem, et solido graviter sonat ungula cornu.
talis, Amyclaei domitus Pollucis habenis,
Cyllarus, et, quorum Graii meminere poëtae,   90
Martis equi biiuges, et magni currus Achilli:
talis et ipse iubam cervice effudit equina,
coniugis adventu pernix, Saturnus, et altum
Pelion hinnitu fugiens implevit acuto.

284–293. *Virgil must hasten on to treat of sheep and goats—a humble subject for poetry but its novelty will carry him on.*

Sed fugit interea, fugit irreparabile tempus,
singula dum capti circumvectamur amore.   285
hoc satis armentis; superat pars altera curae,
lanigeros agitare greges hirtasque capellas.
hic labor; hinc laudem fortes sperate coloni.
nec sum animi dubius, verbis ea vincere magnum
quam sit, et angustis hunc addere rebus honorem.
sed me Parnasi deserta per ardua dulcis   291
raptat amor: iuvat ire iugis, qua nulla priorum
Castaliam molli devertitur orbita clivo.

515–530. *Pestilence among cattle. The ox sorrowing for his yoke-fellow, fallen dead at the plough.*

Ecce autem duro fumans sub vomere taurus   515
concidit, et mixtum spumis vomit ore cruorem,
extremosque ciet gemitus. it tristis arator,
maerentem abiungens fraterna morte iuvencum,
atque opere in medio defixa relinquit aratra.
non umbrae altorum nemorum, non mollia possunt
prata movere animum, non qui per saxa volutus   521
purior electro campum petit amnis: at ima
solvuntur latera, atque oculos stupor urget inertes,
ad terramque fluit devexo pondere cervix.
quid labor aut benefacta iuvant? quid vomere terras
invertisse graves? atqui non Massica Bacchi   526
munera, non illis epulae nocuere repostae:
frondibus et victu pascuntur simplicis herbae;
pocula sunt fontes liquidi atque exercita cursu
flumina; nec somnos abrumpit cura salubres.   530

BOOK IV

1–7. *The little World of the Bees.*

Protinus aerii mellis caelestia dona
exsequar: hanc etiam, Maecenas, adspice partem.
admiranda tibi levium spectacula rerum,
magnanimosque duces, totiusque ordine gentis
mores, et studia, et populos, et proelia, dicam.   5
in tenui labor: at tenuis non gloria, si quem
numina laeva sinunt, auditque vocatus Apollo.

8–50. *Where bee-hives should be placed.*
Delicacy of sense in the bees.

Principio, sedes apibus statioque petenda,
quo neque sit ventis aditus, (nam pabula venti
ferre domum prohibent) neque oves haedique petulci

floribus insultent, aut errans bucula campo   11
decutiat rorem, et surgentes atterat herbas.
absint et picti squalentia terga lacerti
pinguibus a stabulis, meropesque, aliaeque volucres,
et manibus Procne pectus signata cruentis.   15
omnia nam late vastant ipsasque volantes
ore ferunt, dulcem nidis immitibus escam.
at liquidi fontes et stagna virentia musco
adsint, et tenuis fugiens per gramina rivus:
palmaque vestibulum aut ingens oleaster inumbret;
ut, cum prima novi ducent examina reges   21
vere suo, ludetque, favis emissa, iuventus,
vicina invitet decedere ripa calori,
obviaque hospitiis teneat frondentibus arbos.
in medium, seu stabit iners, seu profluet humor,   25
transversas salices et grandia coniice saxa;
pontibus ut crebris possint consistere et alas
pandere ad aestivum solem, si forte morantes
sparserit, aut praeceps Neptuno immerserit Eurus.
haec circum casiae virides, et olentia late   30
serpylla, et graviter spirantis copia thymbrae
floreat, irriguumque bibant violaria fontem.
ipsa autem, seu corticibus tibi suta cavatis,
seu lento fuerint alvaria vimine texta,
angustos habeant aditus: nam frigore mella   35
cogit hiems, eademque calor liquefacta remittit.
utraque vis apibus pariter metuenda; neque illae
nequiquam in tectis certatim tenuia cera
spiramenta linunt, fucoque et floribus oras
explent, collectumque haec ipsa ad munera gluten   40
et visco et Phrygiae servant pice lentius Idae.
saepe etiam effossis, si vera est fama, latebris
sub terra fovere larem, penitusque repertae
pumicibusque cavis exesaeque arboris antro.
tu tamen et levi rimosa cubilia limo   45
ungue fovens circum, et raras super iniice frondes.

neu propius tectis taxum sine, neve rubentes
ure foco cancros, altae neu crede paludi,
aut ubi odor caeni gravis, aut ubi concava pulsu
saxa sonant, vocisque offensa resultat imago.   50

51–66. *In warm weather the bees begin to swarm. How to induce them to settle.*

Quod superest, ubi pulsam hiemem Sol aureus egit
sub terras, caelumque aestiva luce reclusit,
illae continuo saltus silvasque peragrant,
purpureosque metunt flores, et flumina libant
summa leves. hinc nescio qua dulcedine laetae   55
progeniem nidosque fovent; hinc arte recentes
excudunt ceras, et mella tenacia fingunt.
hinc ubi iam emissum caveis ad sidera coeli
nare per aestatem liquidam suspexeris agmen,
obscuramque trahi vento mirabere nubem,   60
contemplator: aquas dulces et frondea semper
tecta petunt. huc tu iussos asperge sapores,
trita melisphylla et cerinthae ignobile gramen;
tinnitusque cie et Matris quate cymbala circum.
ipsae consident medicatis sedibus; ipsae   65
intima more suo sese in cunabula condent.

67–87. *Their heroism in battle.*

Sin autem ad pugnam exierint—nam saepe duobus
regibus incessit magno discordia motu,
continuoque animos volgi, et trepidantia bello
corda, licet longe praesciscere: namque morantes   70
Martius ille aeris rauci canor increpat, et vox
auditur fractos sonitus imitata tubarum;
tum trepidae inter se coëunt, pennisque coruscant,
spiculaque exacuunt rostris, aptantque lacertos,
et circa regem, atque ipsa ad praetoria, densae   75
miscentur, magnisque vocant clamoribus hostem.—

ergo ubi, ver nactae sudum camposque patentes,
erumpunt portis, concurritur; aethere in alto
fit sonitus; magnum mixtae glomerantur in orbem,
praecipitesque cadunt; non densior aëre grando,   80
nec de concussa tantum pluit ilice glandis.
ipsi per medias acies, insignibus alis,
ingentes animos angusto in pectore versant,
usque adeo obnixi non cedere, dum gravis aut hos,
aut hos, versa fuga victor dare terga subegit.   85
hi motus animorum, atque haec certamina tanta,
pulveris exigui iactu compressa, quiescunt.

116–148. *The Pirate turned Market-Gardener.*

Atque equidem, extremo ni iam sub fine laborum
vela traham, et terris festinem advertere proram,
forsitan et, pingues hortos quae cura colendi
ornaret, canerem, biferique rosaria Paesti;
quoque modo potis gauderent intuba rivis,   120
et virides apio ripae, tortusque per herbam
cresceret in ventrem cucumis; nec sera comantem
narcissum, aut flexi tacuissem vimen acanthi,
pallentesque hederas et amantes litora myrtos.
namque sub Oebaliae memini me turribus arcis,   125
qua niger umectat flaventia culta Galaesus,
Corycium vidisse senem, cui pauca relicti
iugera ruris erant; nec fertilis illa iuvencis,
nec pecori opportuna seges nec commoda Baccho.
hic rarum tamen in dumis holus albaque circum   130
lilia verbenasque premens vescumque papaver,
regum aequabat opes animis; seraque revertens
nocte domum dapibus mensas onerabat inemptis.
primus vere rosam atque auctumno carpere poma,
et, cum tristis hiems etiam nunc frigore saxa   135
rumperet, et glacie cursus frenaret aquarum,
ille comam mollis iam tondebat hyacinthi,
aestatem increpitans seram Zephyrosque morantes.

ergo apibus fetis idem atque examine multo
primus abundare, et spumantia cogere pressis   140
mella favis; illi tiliae atque uberrima pinus;
quotque in flore novo pomis se fertilis arbos
induerat, totidem auctumno matura tenebat.
ille etiam seras in versum distulit ulmos,
eduramque pirum et spinos iam pruna ferentes,   145
iamque ministrantem platanum potantibus umbras.
verum haec ipse equidem, spatiis exclusus iniquis
praetereo, atque aliis post me memoranda relinquo.

149-196. *Division of labour among the bees. Each
     works not for himself but for the Community.*

Nunc age, naturas apibus quas Iupiter ipse
addidit, expediam, pro qua mercede, canoros   150
Curetum sonitus crepitantiaque aera secutae,
Dictaeo caeli regem pavere sub antro.
solae communes natos, consortia tecta
urbis habent, magnisque agitant sub legibus aevum;
et patriam solae et certos novere penates;   155
venturaeque hiemis memores aestate laborem
experiuntur, et in medium quaesita reponunt.
namque aliae victu invigilant et foedere pacto
exercentur agris; pars intra saepta domorum
narcissi lacrimam et lentum de cortice gluten,   160
prima favis ponunt fundamina, deinde tenaces
suspendunt ceras; aliae, spem gentis, adultos
educunt fetus; aliae purissima mella
stipant, et liquido distendunt nectare cellas.
sunt, quibus ad portas cecidit custodia sorti;   165
inque vicem speculantur aquas et nubila coeli;
aut onera accipiunt venientum, aut agmine facto
ignavum, fucos, pecus a praesepibus arcent.
fervet opus, redolentque thymo fragrantia mella.
ac veluti lentis Cyclopes fulmina massis   170
cum properant, alii taurinis follibus auras

accipiunt redduntque, alii stridentia tinguunt
aera lacu; gemit impositis incudibus Aetna:
illi inter sese magna vi brachia tollunt
in numerum, versantque tenaci forcipe ferrum: 175
non aliter, si parva licet componere magnis,
Cecropias innatus apes amor urguet habendi,
munere quamque suo. grandaevis oppida curae,
et munire favos et daedala fingere tecta:
at fessae multâ referunt se nocte minores,   180
crura thymo plenae; pascuntur et arbuta passim,
et glaucas salices casiamque crocumque rubentem,
et pinguem tiliam et ferrugineos hyacinthos.
omnibus una quies operum, labor omnibus unus.
mane ruunt portis; nusquam mora: rursus, easdem
vesper ubi e pastu tandem decedere campis   186
admonuit, tum tecta petunt, tum corpora curant;
fit sonitus, mussantque oras et limina circum.
post, ubi iam thalamis se composuere, siletur
in noctem, fessosque sopor suus occupat artus.   190
nec vero a stabulis, pluvia impendente, recedunt
longius, aut credunt caelo adventantibus Euris:
sed circum tutae sub moenibus urbis aquantur,
excursusque breves tentant, et saepe lapillos,
ut cumbae instabiles, fluctu iactante, saburram,   195
tollunt: his sese per inania nubila librant.

210–218. *They will die in battle for their King.*

Praeterea, regem non sic Aegyptos et ingens   210
Lydia, nec populi Parthorum, aut Medus Hydaspes,
observant. rege incolumi, mens omnibus una est;
amisso, rupere fidem, constructaque mella
diripuere ipsae et crates solvere favorum.
ille operum custos: illum admirantur, et omnes   215
circumstant fremitu denso stipantque frequentes;
et saepe attollunt humeris, et corpora bello
obiectant pulchramque petunt per vulnera mortem.

219–227. Such human attributes, their industry, obedience to law and loyalty to their King, prove that the bees inherit a special portion of the Divine Intelligence which is the source of all life.

His quidam signis, atque haec exempla secuti,
esse apibus partem divinae mentis, et haustus   220
aetherios, dixere: Deum namque ire per omnes
terrasque tractusque maris caelumque profundum.
hinc pecudes, armenta, viros, genuš omne ferarum,
quemque sibi tenues nascentem arcessere vitas:
scilicet huc reddi deinde, ac resoluta referri   225
omnia; nec morti esse locum; sed viva volare
sideris in numerum atque alto succedere caelo.

453–470. The Story of Orpheus. Death of Eurydice. Her husband follows her down to Erebus.

Non te nullius exercent numinis irae;
magna luis commissa: tibi has miserabilis Orpheus
haud quaquam ob meritum poenas, ni fata resistant
suscitat et rapta graviter pro coniuge saevit.   456
illa quidem, dum te fugeret per flumina praeceps,
immanem ante pedes hydrum moritura puella,
servantem ripas, alta non vidit in herba.
at chorus aequalis Dryadum clamore supremos   460
implerunt montes; flerunt Rhodopeïae arces,
altaque Pangaea et Rhesi Mavortia tellus,
atque Getae, atque Hebrus, et Actias Orithyia.
ipse, cava solans aegrum testudine amorem,
te, dulcis coniunx, te solo in littore secum,   465
te veniente die, te decedente, canebat.
Taenarias etiam fauces, alta ostia Ditis,
et caligantem nigra formidine lucum,
ingressus, Manesque adiit, regemque tremendum,
nesciaque humanis precibus mansuescere corda.   470

*471-503. The spirits of the dead flock to listen to his
singing. Even Pluto is struck with pity and allows
Eurydice to return to life. But Orpheus breaks the
covenant with Pluto, looks back and she is lost to him.*

At, cantu commotae, Erebi de sedibus imis
umbrae ibant tenues simulacraque luce carentum:
quam multa in foliis avium se millia condunt,
vesper ubi aut hibernus agit de montibus imber;
matres, atque viri, defunctaque corpora vita   475
magnanimûm heroum, pueri, innuptaeque puellae,
impositique rogis iuvenes ante ora parentum:
quos circum limus niger, et deformis harundo
Cocyti, tardaque palus inamabilis unda
adligat, et novies Styx interfusa coërcet.   480
quin ipsae stupuere domus atque intima Leti
Tartara, caeruleosque implexae crinibus angues
Eumenides, tenuitque inhians tria Cerberus ora,
atque Ixionii vento rota constitit orbis.
iamque, pedem referens, casus evaserat omnes,   485
redditaque Eurydice superas veniebat ad auras,
pone sequens; namque hanc dederat Proserpina legem;
cum subita incautum dementia cepit amantem,
ignoscenda quidem, scirent si ignoscere Manes:
restitit, Eurydicenque suam iam luce sub ipsa,   490
immemor, heu! victusque animi, respexit. ibi omnis
effusus labor, atque immitis rupta tyranni
foedera, terque fragor stagnis auditus Avernis.
illa, Quis et me, inquit, miseram, et te perdidit,
    Orpheu,
quis tantus furor? en! iterum crudelia retro   495
fata vocant conditque natantia lumina somnus.
iamque vale: feror ingenti circumdata nocte,
invalidasque tibi tendens, heu! non tua, palmas.
dixit, et ex oculis subito, ceu fumus in auras
commixtus tenues, fugit diversa; neque illum,   500

prensantem nequiquam umbras, et multa volentem
dicere, praeterea vidit; nec portitor Orci
amplius obiectam passus transire paludem.

504–527. *His lamentations and wanderings.*

Quid faceret? quo se, rapta bis coniuge, ferret?
quo fletu manes, qua numina voce moveret?   505
illa quidem Stygia nabat iam frigida cymba.
septem illum totos perhibent ex ordine menses
rupe sub aëria deserti ad Strymonis undam
flevisse et gelidis haec evolvisse sub antris,
mulcentem tigres et agentem carmine quercus: 510
qualis populea maerens philomela sub umbra
amissos queritur fetus, quos durus arator
observans nido implumes detraxit: at illa
flet noctem, ramoque sedens miserabile carmen
integrat, et maestis late loca questibus implet.   515
nulla Venus, non ulli animum flexere hymenaei;
solus Hyperboreas glacies Tanaïmque nivalem,
arvaque Rhipaeis nunquam viduata pruinis
lustrabat, raptam Eurydicen atque irrita Ditis
dona querens: spretae Ciconum quo munere matres,
inter sacra deum nocturnique orgia Bacchi,   521
discerptum latos iuvenem sparsere per agros.
tum quoque, marmorea caput a cervice revulsum
gurgite cum medio portans Oeagrius Hebrus
volveret, 'Eurydicen' vox ipsa et frigida lingua, 525
'ah miseram Eurydicen!' anima fugiente vocabat;
'Eurydicen' toto referebant flumine ripae.

559–566. *While Virgil has been writing the Georgics
Augustus is fighting for his country in the East.*

Haec super arvorum cultu pecorumque canebam,
et super arboribus, Caesar dum magnus ad altum
fulminat Euphraten bello, victorque volentes   561
per populos dat iura, viamque affectat Olympo.
illo Virgilium me tempore dulcis alebat
Parthenope, studiis florentem ignobilis otî:
carmina qui lusi pastorum, audaxque iuventa,   565
Tityre, te patulae cecini sub tegmine fagi.

NOTES

GEORGIC I

1–5

Virgil begins by describing the subjects of the four *Georgics*. Agriculture, the care of fruit trees and vines, of horses and cattle, and lastly bee-keeping. He goes on to invoke all the Gods who are guardians of the country and its occupations, the Sun and Moon who bring the seasons, Bacchus and Ceres, also the lesser deities of field and forest, the Fauns, Dryads and Silvanus, also Neptune, the creator of the horse, Pan the tender of sheep, Minerva who gave man the olive and so on. The invocation of these heavenly Powers who care for the husbandman is natural and beautiful. He then proceeds to invoke the aid of the Emperor, not yet a God but destined to become one.

1. **quid...segetes,** 'what makes the corn-fields glad.' The Latin metaphor should be preserved. It was borrowed by Virgil from the speech of the country-folk: *laetas segetes etiam rustici dicunt* (Cic. *De Or.* III, 155). As Sidgwick says, "This opening phrase strikes the key-note of the poem." To Virgil the luxuriant fields have a joy of their own. "The poet had in an unusual degree the true Italian feeling that there is something mysterious or divine in all life, even in that of plants—a feeling at the root of the religion of the early Italians" (Dr W. Warde Fowler). **quo sidere,** 'at the rising of what constellation.'

2. **Maecenas,** the prime-minister of Augustus who was both patron and friend of Virgil and Horace.

4. **pecori, apibus.** Note the hiatus. Datives of the object or work contemplated.

5. **hinc,** 'from this point of time,' 'I will now essay.'

71–83

71. **alternis,** 'every other year,' abl. plur. neut. of *alternus* used as an adverb. Note the emphatic position of the word. **idem...patiere,** 'moreover, you will allow your reaped fallows to rest.' The meaning of *novales* is strained, for the fields were not fallow till they had ceased to grow crops; the word is used proleptically.

76. **silvam sonantem,** 'the rustling haulm,' i.e. the dry stalks of the gathered beans and peas. *Silva* seems a gardener's term for the luxurant stems of plants, as at *G.* I, 152, and IV, 273.

77. **urit,** 'exhausts,' takes the substance out of, as does fire

79–81. Note the position of *arida* and *effetos* and also C.'s rendering, 'Yet rotation will lighten the strain: only think of the dried-up soil and do not be afraid to give it its fill of rich manure—think of the exhausted field,' etc.

81. **cinerem,** 'wood-ashes,' used as a top-dressing.

83. The soil is not 'thankless' in its return as when left fallow

118–146

118–146. This passage is a summary of man's progress in the arts, as described in the end of Lucretius' fifth book. But the idea of a benevolent purpose for which Providence has imposed toil on man is Virgil's own. The ethic of the passage is thoroughly Virgilian, and is distinctive of the *Georgics* as a poem.

118. **nec...nihil,** like *haud facilem* in l. 122, means the opposite of 'harmless' or 'easy.' Thus in English, 'no small' is stronger than 'great.'

119. **improbus,** 'tormenting,' 'pestilent.' As *probus* implies moderation, especially in respect for others' rights, so *improbus* means 'unscrupulous,' 'rapacious,' and is even applied to things as at l. 146. Cf. Martial XII, 18 *ingenti fruor improboque somno,* of a 'huge' prolonged sleep. The epithet, 'the *pestilent* goose,' expressing the farmer's irritation, is an instance of the playfulness which is characteristic of the *Georgics*. So at l. 182 V. speaks of the 'tiny mouse building a mansion and a granary underground' and of the 'ant fearing an old age of poverty': at l. 160 he speaks of the husbandman's tools as his 'weapons' in a hand-to-hand fight with Nature (ll. 104–5). See Sidgwick, vol. I, p. 39.

120. **Strymoniae,** from the river Strymon in Macedon, where cranes abounded; often mentioned in Greek poets. This is called 'a literary epithet.' It has no descriptive force. It makes the poetry of a thing consist in its associations more than in the thing itself, and is therefore more or less artificial in point of style. The Augustan poets are fond of such epithets. Thus we have 'Paphian myrtle' at II, 64; 'Chaonian acorns' at l. 8; 'Cecropian thyme' at IV, 177, where see note.

121. **ipse** added to the name of a god seems to express dignity, 'the great Father himself,' as well as purpose and personal intervention. In the *Georgics*, Virgil generally uses the term 'Pater,' to denote the supreme spiritual Power.

122. **per artem,** 'by system,' on a scientific method.

123. **corda,** in older Latin 'the wits,' 'the intellect.'

125. **ante Iovem,** in the Saturnian or 'Golden Age,' when Saturn, the father of Jupiter, reigned in Latium.

126. 'Even to set a mark on the land or divide it with a boundary-line was a thing unlawful,' C. The Romans generally divided land into rectangular sections, the corners of which were marked by boundary-stones. *Limes* is often used in the latter sense. Cf. *Aen.* xii, 898.

127. **in medium**, 'for the common stock'; **ipsa**, 'of her own accord.'

129. **serpentibus...atris**. Dr W. Fowler remarks that Virgil uses *ater* to convey a sense of ghastliness or dreadfulness, rather than simply the meaning 'black' (*Death of Turnus*, pp. 78, 92). 'Black' has similar associations in English.

131. Honey was believed to fall on the leaves from heaven in the form of dew. See iv, 1. **removit**, 'took away' (see l. 135). Virgil ignores the legend of fire brought down from heaven in a stem of fennel by Prometheus. This jarred with his own standpoint; he leaves fire to be discovered by human ingenuity.

133–4. Notice the force of *extunderet*, 'might hammer out.' **paulatim**, emphatic by position.

138. **Pleiadas**. The short final syllable is lengthened at times, but only in the first syllable of the foot, that on which the ictus falls, and especially before a pause in the verse. C. considers *h* to have the force of a consonant. The daughter of Lycaon, Callisto, was loved by Jupiter, but changed by Juno into a bear (*arctos* in Greek), and transformed by Jupiter into the Constellation of the Great Bear or the Plough.

142. **alta**, 'the bottom,' which a casting-net requires to reach.

143. **rigor ferri**, 'stubborn iron.' Probably also the abstract expression is preferred to the concrete, in order to intensify the stern associations of the sword. **argutus**, participle of *arguo* (from a root *arg*, meaning 'white' in Greek; seen in the Latin *argentum* 'the white or bright metal'). *Arguo* means first to 'make a thing bright' then to 'make evident' or 'prove'; so with *clarus*, 'bright or shining,' and *de-claro*, 'to make evident' to the mind, the English 'clear' being also used in this double sense. Kennedy in his note on *Ecl.* vii, 1 says: "The adjective is used of things which convey a clear perception and has many shades of meaning (fine, minute, sharp, shrewd-speaking, melodious, loud, shrill, etc.)." Thus at l. 294 it is used of the ringing sound of the weaver's comb, at 377 of the swallow, at *Ecl.* vii of the rustling oaks, here of the 'shrill' saw, also by other writers of a 'pungent' smell or taste, by Cicero in the sense 'acute,' 'witty.'

146. **improbus**, 'relentless': see note on l. 119. **omnia**, 'all obstacles.' 'Want that grinds (harries) amid hardship.' Cf.

Caesar cum legionem ab hostibus urgeri vidisset, B. G. II, 26; *urgent Teucer te, te Sthenelus,* Hor. *C.* I, 15. 23.

147–168

148. **iam…deficerent,** 'began to fail.' **silvae,** probably dat. of indirect object (C. takes it as genitive), referring to the famous oak-forest of Dodona in Epirus, regarded as the first dwelling of the human race.

150. 'Soon however the corn-crop too acquired troubles of its own,' i.e. troubles for the farmer: *ut* is explanatory. **frumenta,** plur., is used specially in the sense of 'standing grain.'

151. **segnis carduus,** 'the lazy thistle.' Transference of epithet. See n. on IV, 50.

152. **silva** used to denote the vigour of the weed-crop: 'a prickly jungle,' C.

154. **dominantur,** 'lord it among the glistening corn': the verb at once calls up such weeds towering above the wheat. **s. avenae,** 'wild oats'; oats were not cultivated by Romans or Greeks.

155. **quod,** used especially before *si* or *nisi* to mark the connection with what precedes. 'So unless.'

156. 'Of the darkened field.' Notice C.'s rendering, 'unless your hook is ever ready to exterminate weeds, your shout to scare away birds,' etc., which brings out the emphasis on the ablatives *rastris, sonitu, falce, votis,* by making them subjects in each clause.

158. **heu,** 'poor man,' C.

160. **duris,** 'sturdy.' **arma,** 'weapons.' By many such touches V. treats the husbandman's labour as a warfare: the poet knew well what adverse forces he has to combat, and the hardness of his life. Cf. *imperat arvis,* ll. 99 and 145–6.

162. **primum** includes *vomis.*

163. **tarda volventia,** the adj. qualifies the present participle with adverbial force. V. uses many such transitive verbs as *volvo* intransitively, e.g. *sisto* at l. 479, *addo,* probably, at 513, *Aen.* VII, 27 *venti posuere,* 'the winds fell.' **matris.** Demeter goddess of agriculture, identified with Ceres, was worshipped at Eleusis in Attica.

164. **iniquo,** 'cruel,' lit. 'immoderate.' **tribulum,** 'a threshing-sledge,' a plank studded with sharp stones or iron, dragged by cattle over the corn. **trahea,** a similar instrument on wheels. See K. *Terms of Husbandry.*

165. **Celeus,** son of Triptolemus, who invented the plough. **virgea supellex,** 'baskets,' 'hurdles,' etc.

166. **mystica v.** The winnowing-fan, entitled 'mystic'

because it was carried in the processions at the Eleusinian Mysteries.

167. 'All which you will remember to store up long before the day of need,' C.

168. 'digna might mean "the full glory," i.e. glory such as would be worth ambition,' C. divini ruris: to V. rural life has associations of special sacredness.

193–203

193. The farmer must combat the tendency of things to degenerate. semina, 'as for pulse,' i.e. leguminous plants as seen from *siliquis*, l. 195. medicare prius, 'first pickle' or steep it in soda before sowing it: νίτρον, carbonate of soda not, like our 'nitre,' saltpetre, according to L. and S.

195. fallacibus, because, says Keightley, 'the pod is of the same size whether the beans are large or small.'

196. maderent, 'be boiled quickly.' properata = *propere*: Plautus uses *madeo*, 'to be cooked,' lit. 'to be sodden.' Various writers *de re rustica* state that steeping before sowing makes beans cook more easily. quamvis, here an adverb qualifying *exiguo*.

197. 'Spite of all patience in choosing, spite of all pains in examining,' C. diu refers to carrying out the process for years. Page says: "Artificial selection, such as Virgil recommends, is the cause of the immense improvement in all our domesticated seeds, and unless this is continually practised, the plant will revert to the character of its wild ancestor."

198. vis humana, 'human effort.' Lucretius uses the same phrase at v, 206 in describing the farmer's constant struggle with nature. But Virgil views this struggle with a different eye, and with a noble submission to the discipline it involves.

199. 'Thus all things are doomed to speed to the worse and to slide back and degenerate.' ruere and referri are historical infinitives used to express what occurs habitually. *Ruere ac retro sublapsa referri* is pleonastic, a strong instance of what S. calls "accumulated expression," frequent in Virgil; so *reddi ac resoluta referri* at *G.* IV, 225, *sollicitam timor anxius angit* at *Aen.* IX, 89. Note the marked alliteration in 200, suggesting the continued sliding back, also in 203, Praeceps prono rapit alveus amni.

203. Aulus Gellius, who writes in the second century A.D., and Servius, whom Keightley follows, make *atque = statim*. Few editors accept this: most consider the two clauses with *subigit* and *rapit* as parallel without any apodosis. atque is

certainly used of one event following close upon another as at Catullus LXV, 23, 'And lo! the current whirls him away.' *illum* refers strictly to *lembum*, comparing the seed degenerating to the boat which is carried down: but the boat implies the rower: **alveus**, strictly 'the channel' which suggests 'the current.'

This doctrine is sometimes quoted as 'pessimistic.' Rather is it the opposite. Virgil is showing how in the hard wrestle with Nature man can conquer.

259-275

260. **forent properanda**, 'would require to be done in haste.' **coelo sereno** is equal to a clause with *si*. **maturo** combines the meanings 'to do a thing early' and 'to do it with full consideration.'

261. **procudit**, 'hammers at the point,' i.e. 'sharpens,' cf. Lucr. v, 1265 *in acuta et tenuia posse Mucronum duci fastigia procudendo*, of beating out masses of metal into sharp tools.

262. **lintres**, 'troughs' for holding grapes.

263. **acervis**, 'heaps' extended into the sense of 'sacks.'

264. **furcas bicornes**, 'forked props,' to help the vines to climb up the elms, as explained in *G.* II, 359.

265. **Amerina**, the town of Ameria in Umbria seems to have been famous for its willows.

266. **facilis**, more properly applied to *virga*.

268. **quippe** corroborates a statement or justifies it as here. 'Nay even religion and its ordinances.' By the words *fas et iura*, as Dr Fowler says, "V. undoubtedly means the action of the pontifices in making or relaxing rules." Following Servius the two words are usually explained to mean religious and civil law respectively. "But it is certain that the pontifices alone had cognisance of these rules and their *ius pontificium* was part of the *ius divinum* which governed all religious matters. V. adopts the term *fas*, then just coming to be used in this sense, to mean this pontifical law and adds *iura* to make it more intelligible." *fas*, originally an adjective, in course of time took on the character of a substantive.

269. **deducere** might mean either 'to let off' or as at l. 113 'to let on' the water to a field. The former might be necessary either in case of overflow or to irrigate the fields of a neighbour. Much jealousy has existed in Italy regarding the amount of time during which each farmer can use the water-supply.

The *dies festi* or *feriae* were days made over to the Gods and kept holy by resting on them. The exceptions made by V. show the practical good-sense of the Roman. The famous pontiff,

Mucius Scaevola, when asked what occupations were permitted on such days, replied, 'Anything the neglect of which might cause harm.' Irrigation might naturally come under this rule. Light work was permitted but no new undertaking might be commenced. Sheep-washing might be performed casually as a remedy for scab but not as the important annual operation. Recreation was lawful, such as bird-catching or a visit to town to barter goods. Cicero says that such days were specially ordained as holidays for slaves. See Dr Fowler's article "The Law of Rest-Days" in *Roman Essays*, 1920.

270. **religio** here in the negative sense, 'a restraining principle,' 'a religious scruple.' The etymology is uncertain. Cicero derives it from *re-legere*, 'to ponder earnestly,' in spite of *re* being short (though the occasional spelling *relligio*, which lengthens it, may represent an original *red-ligio*). In spite of *i* in *ligo* being long, Servius and others derive it from *religare* which Lucretius' well-known line *religionum animum nodis exsolvere pergo* seems to support. Since Lucretius can see in religion only the sense of fear which he feels to be degrading, naturally he uses the word to denote 'superstition,' including both awe before the unknown powers and organised worship in all its forms. In the pre-Christian Latin writers *religio* is not a virtue in the same sense as *pietas* but is properly a feeling of uneasiness or fear which may or may not be viewed as prompting true religious feeling and worship.

270. 'To plant a hedge beside the corn.'

272. **balantum** is here forcible, as sheep bleat when they are washed. **salubri**, emphatic, implies when dipping is needed for the health of the sheep.

273. **agitator**, the farmer himself is meant. Varro observes that markets were held as holy days to give countrymen an opportunity of going into town.

275. **incusum**, 'dented,' i.e. 'roughened' or 'grooved,' so as better to crush the corn. For this reason Roman mill-stones found in England are often formed of rough volcanic stone from the Eifel.

287–310

287. **adeo** strongly emphasizes the preceding word. Virgil is very fond of placing it as second word in a sentence in this use. 'Nay there are many things which allow themselves to be performed better.' **dedere**, the perfect used instead of the present to express a recurring action, hence called the 'gnomic perfect' from its use in maxims, cf. *G.* IV, 213–14. Note the fourfold repetition of *nox* in ll. 287–290, the object of this

somewhat rhetorical artifice being to emphasize the importance of certain times for given operations. See P.'s note.

288. **Eous**, adjective from *Eōs*, 'dawn' used as a noun ='Lucifer,' the morning star (ἀστήρ masc. being understood).

289. **stipulae**, Varro says that the ancient method of reaping was to cut off the heads of the corn, either close or half-way to the ear and leave the straw to be cut afterwards. This would be easiest when the corn was wet with the dew. Cf. the use of *stringere* at 305 and 317, also Keightley's *Terms of Husbandry* under 'Messis.'

290. **lentus** really applies to the grass. The moisture makes the grass soft and pliant so that the sickle catches hold.

291. **et quidam**, 'I know a man who will sit the whole night through,' C. V. is apparently thinking of some crofter known to him, but *quidam* might also mean 'one,' τις, as a sample of a class; we seem to have a Virgilian inversion, *luminis* and *ignis* changing meaning, 'by the light of the winter fire till late in the night.' If *lumen* is rendered 'a lamp,' the epithet *hiberni* loses its force: *ignes* could hardly mean the flame of a lamp.

294. **arguto**, 'tuneful' or 'shrill.' P. says: "The comb is as its name implies a bar of wood, provided with teeth which are inserted between the threads of the warp and then by a sharp upward (or downward) movement the instrument is used to drive the cross-threads of the woof close together, thus making the texture firm." Aristophanes in the *Frogs* speaks of the 'singing shuttle.' See P.'s explanation of the process at l. 285.

295-6. **decoquit humorem et**. "Notice hypermetric line suggesting the boiling over of the must," P. It is very questionable whether any such intention is to be seen here.

mustum, "the sweet grape juice boiled down to jelly....It was preserved from fermentation by boiling....*Mustum* is strictly the sweet juice of the grape before it has undergone any chemical change, although the word is sometimes used loosely for wine," Ramsay, *Roman Antiquities*, pp. 438-9.

296. **trepidi**, 'bubbling' properly belongs to *undam*.

297-8. **rubicunda Ceres**, 'the corn when it is growing brown.' **medio aestu** seems to mean 'in mid-day heat' (P. and Pap. render thus), C. renders 'in midsummer heat' since midday is precisely the time for the reaper to rest. Theocr. x, 49 advises reapers to avoid the heat of mid-day, but he writes of Sicily where the climate is far hotter than in V.'s country. But in the same passage Theocritus advises to thresh the corn at mid-day since the heat helps to loosen the kernel from the chaff and this practice is still followed in Northern

Italy. On the whole the meaning 'mid-day heat,' though less plausible, seems justified here. "It is obvious that the contrast here is between *day*-time and *night*-time," Pap. The contrast with winter does not properly begin till l. 299.

299. **nudus** means discarding the outer garment as Cincinnatus had done when the Senate's messages found him. *Nudus* is not to be taken literally, though Servius has a story that a wag finished the line with the words *habebis frigora, febrem* (perhaps *frigore* should be read here).

302. 'Merry winter bids the guest,' **genialis**, 'calling out man's happier self,' C. The genius is a sort of second self which is born along with each of us. It expressed the individuality of a man: the idea of a man's self, the happier and impulsive part of him [hence its significance in English as the special gift which enables a writer to express his own personality]. The Genius participates specially in our pleasures and was worshipped on birthdays and holidays. W. Warde Fowler, *R.E.R.* p. 75. Hence *indulgere Genio* means 'to enjoy oneself.' **resolvit**, 'unbinds.'

305. **tamen**, though winter is a festive time, 'still.'

309. 'With a vigorous whirl of the hempen lash of your B. sling.' P. who explains *verbera* as the bullet hurled, says, "The whole expression is highly artificial," but *verbera* is used ='thongs' as in Ovid, *Met.* VII, 777 *excussae contorto verbere glandes.*

316–335

317. **iam stringeret**, 'was beginning to strip off the ears of barley from the brittle stalk': see n. on 289. **fragili culmo** is not, I think, a descriptive ablative with *hordea*.

318. 'I have seen all the armies of the winds meet in the shock of battle,' C., who says, "the winds are supposed to be blowing from all quarters at once." He also compares Daniel vii, 2 "The four winds of heaven strove upon the great sea." **omnia proelia ventorum** seems to be used for *proelia omnium ventorum.*

319–21. **quae...eruerent**. Subj. expresses the result, 'so as to tear up.' Note the repetition of *ex* in *expulsam eruerent.* The 'accumulated expression,' as S. points out, is one characteristic of V.'s style: see on l. 200. **ita**. What is the relation of the two clauses with *eruerent* and *ferret*? C. takes them as contrasted; the violent summer storm tears up acres of heavy corn by the root as easily as 'a common hurricane' would sweep away light straw and flying stubble. Kennedy, followed by P. and Pap., makes both clauses refer to the same tempest: *ita* being ='when uprooted' and might be rendered 'and then,' while *ferret* continues the construction of *eruerent*. Kennedy renders 'and then with black eddy the storm whirled the light branches and flying straws,' i.e. first it tears up the barley by the roots and carries it high into the air, then with eddying currents whirls it round and round in that situation. Thus we have a complete picture, exhibiting the singular violence and strength of the hurricane.

322–6 describe a cloud-burst, the preceding sentence a hurricane: *agmen aquarum* being contrasted with *omnia ventorum proelia*.

323. 'The clouds mustering from the length and breadth of heaven, and making their dark storms into one great murky tempest; down crashes the whole dome of the firmament and washes away,' C. **glomerant**, used often of soldiers mustering in close fighting, keeps up the metaphor of *agmen aquarum*.

324. **ruit aether**, so *caeli ruina* in *Aen.* I, 129, of a downpour. 'The sky pours sheer down,' Mackail. **ex alto**, 'from on high' or 'off the sea.' K. prefers the latter, "for the clouds which bear rain, always ascend from the horizon."

326. **cava** because in summer there is little or no water in the Italian rivers: "they resemble a road running between two high banks," K.

327. **fretis spirantibus**,. 'the sea boils through its panting firths'; the violent heaving of the waves being compared to the hard breathing of a man making a great effort. Cf. *Aen.* x, 291, *qua vada non spirant* of Tarchon finding a shallow place where the sea does not break with violence, 'does not seethe,' C. One might compare with these two instances the following from a writer of the day: "The sailors gazed at the ominous sky and the equally ominous sea that breathed in long, low, ominous undulations" (Jack London in *A Son of the Sun*, p. 153). This writer was certainly not imitating Virgil.

328. **ipse Pater**, 'the great Father himself, entrenched in a night of storm-clouds, wields the huge thunderbolts with flashing arm,' C.

329. **molitur**, V. is fond of using this word for any action accompanied with effort or difficulty (C. gives its value by adding 'huge'). **motu**, the shock of the thunderbolt.

330–1. **fugere, stravit**, not here the gnomic aorist but the perfect of instantaneous action for which compare the three perfects at *G.* IV, 213–14. But Kennedy prefers to render,

> Beasts have fled
> And mortal hearts, the world throughout, have sunk
> In crouching palpitation. He the while, etc.

assuming that all living things have already gone into hiding from the storm. **fugere...et stravit.** "The two perfects connected by *et* apparently describe actions connected and simultaneous" while the disconnected clauses describe successive effects, C.

331. **per gentes,** 'all over the world men's hearts lie quailing low with terror.' We may compare Lucr. v, 1218–25, *populi gentesque tremunt,* whole realms awed by the thunder-storm.

332. **Athŏn** as if from nom. *Athŏs. Athō* is the correct accus. form, from Ἄθως. The adjective Acroceraunia, used as noun, means 'heights of thunder' (κεραυνός, 'a thunderbolt') which V. renders *alta Ceraunia.* These famous mountains were on the Adriatic in Epirus. The coast skirting them was specially dangerous to ships.

333. **deiicit,** strictly 'casts down' (of a rock), here extended in meaning to 'strikes.' "The dactylic pause is effective in such a place but more so still the monosyllabic, obtainable in Greek and English poetry," says Kennedy who compares *Iliad* I, 51–2 and *Paradise Lost,* XI, 491:

> And over them triumphant Death his dart
> Shook—but delayed to strike.

ingeminant, 'louder and louder roar the South winds and ever thicker falls the rain'; after a peal of thunder rain and wind generally increase. Cf. Lucr. v, 289, *Quo de concussu* (comp. *quo motu* above) *sequitur gravis imber et uber.* **Austri,** note that Auster is the proper Latin name for the South wind, not Notus, borrowed from the Greek, which is vague and may mean any wind. (W. Warde Fowler, *Class. Rev.* June, 1908.)

334. 'Under the mighty blast now the woods and again the shores wail in agony,' *plangunt* being used with *nunc—nunc,* 'by turns,' intransitively as at *Aen.* XI, 145, instead of the passive.

322–34. Kennedy writes: "The elaborate splendour of these lines is surpassed by no other passage in Virgil. The pause at *dextra* marks the calmness of conscious strength; at *tremit,* breathless terror; at *pavor,* prostrate expectation. The following *ille* and the thrice repeated *aut* express the majestic ease of omnipotence; at *deicit* falls the sudden crash of the bolt; in the words which follow is heard the rushing, struggling, moaning tempest."

Note the alliterations at 329 and 330. The variety of the pauses throughout this passage should be specially noticed. See Introduction, p. xlv

351–382

351. haec, i.e. *aestus, pluvia*, etc.

353. 'What warnings the moon in her monthly course was to give us; what should betoken a fall of the wind.'

354. 'What sign, if they see it repeated, should make the husbandmen keep,' etc.

356. continuo, 'from the first,' i.e. the moment the wind is getting up. *Continuo* is used of some event which follows without interval another introduced by *ubi, postquam*, etc. "Virgil is also fond of placing this as first word in a sentence and defining the time to which it refers afterwards" as at l. 60, followed by *quo tempore*. P. **freta,** 'the inlets,' firths.

356–9. Here as always in Virgil, the adaptation of metre to sense is impressive: at l. 357 *incipiunt agitata tumescere*, the rapid dactylic verse movement, to express the disturbance of the sea, the abrupt noise of crashing branches from the forest, and, following the sharp pause after *fragor*, the full unbroken cadence which marks the storm at its height. But we must not carry the notion of conscious intent too far when regarding this adaptation of metre to meaning.

Aut is not intended to disjoin the two classes of storm-tokens; it merely indicates that in case sea or mountains or forests be not near enough for observation, all the signs will somewhere occur.

359. misceri, another favourite word of V.'s expressing anything disorderly or noisy. The notion of 'confusion' passes easily into that of 'riot' or 'noise.' Here it should be rendered by a noun—'a confused roar echoes far along the beach,' C. *Misceri* properly applies to the sound not the shore.

360. temperat sibi male, 'hardly restrains itself from injuring the ships': *temperat sibi = parcit*, C. *Tempero* is used with ablative in Livy and Tacitus.

361. mergi, according to K. 'gulls': *mergus* is often rendered 'cormorant.' But, as Keightley says, the cormorant does not fly to land thus before a storm. "The only bird to which this description will properly apply is the sea-gull."

362–4. marinae. Both the word and its position are emphatic, 'the cormorants whose element is the water.' **notas,** 'its home in the marsh.'

368. frondes caducas, leaves either 'fallen' or 'fluttering about as they fall,' *Aen.* VI, 481 supports the former, and X, 622 the latter sense.

369. 'Or feathers that float on the surface of a pool, huddling together.' **plumas** is not 'gossamer' but feathers dropped from ducks, etc. Aratus, 189, makes thistle-down playing on the water a sign of wind.

370–3. **fulminat de parte**, 'when lightning comes from the quarter.' The sentence means that thunder from whatever quarter it comes is a sign of rain. **domus**, as if each of the winds had a home in the quarter it blows from. **rura**, 'the fields.'

373–4. **imprudentibus**, 'without warning,' lit. 'not foreseeing it.' **obfuit**, in a bad sense, 'surprises men.' Aristotle too says that cranes descend before rain.

375. 'The soaring cranes take refuge from the storm in the depth of the valleys,' C. The close conjunction of *aëriae* and *vallibus imis* seems to imply contrast. See Royds, p. 36.

377. **arguta**, 'twittering.' Here twittering is also a sign of rain. The *hirundo* included all the different species of Martin and Swallow (*A Year with the Birds*, p. 250).

378. **veterem querelam**, 'their immemorial croak,' 'their old complaining note.'

380. **bibit arcus**. The rainbow was supposed to draw up moisture from the sea, rivers, etc., and to discharge it in rain.

393–423

393–4. 'Not less sure are the signs by which you may foresee and learn a change from rain to sunshine,' C. **soles**, sunny days as at Ovid, *Trist.* v, 8–31 *si numeres anno soles et nubila toto*. **serena**, used as subst. Cf. *tranquilla alta* when *alta* is subst. at *Aen.* II, 203.

395. **acies**, 'keen edge.' **obtusa**, 'blurred,' P.

396. **obnoxia**, 'under obligation,' 'indebted.' It is a good sign if the moon and stars are brilliant, and have not what sailors term 'a sickly look.'

397. **tenuia**, see n. on l. 482.

398. **tepidum**, 'the afternoon or evening sun,' C.

399. **alcyon**, here certainly the kingfisher (*A Year with the Birds*, by Dr Warde Fowler, p. 240). The Greeks seem to have thought of the Halcyon mainly as a sea-bird (*ibid.* p. 241). Dr Fowler tells us that it is at home on the sea-shore as V. here represents, but instead of being a singer as described at *G.* III, 338, it is "a silent bird."

400. **solutos iactare maniplos**, 'to shake out their litter and toss it up,' M.

401. **nebulae**, the clouds on the mountains.

403. **exercet noctua cantus**. The verb which means 'to keep

busy,' 'keep on at' a thing, admirably describes the persistent
hooting of the owl, which is supposed to be calling down bad
weather. **noctua**, probably means the small owl which was
sacred to Athena. It is not indigenous to Britain but was
introduced from Italy last century. As V. here implies, it
begins to hoot before sunset. Royds, p. 45.

404. **apparet**. This verb is repeatedly placed at the beginning of a line by Virgil, where he wishes to emphasize some
sight of special pathos or significance, e.g. at *Aen.* I, 118
apparent rari nantes in gurgite vasto, of two or three swimmers
seen after a ship has foundered; II, 483–4, in two successive
lines, of the sacred halls of Priam's royal palace exposed to
public view after the Greeks have burst in; II, 623, when
Aeneas' eyes have been opened to see the Gods hostile to Troy,
leading on the enemy at the fall of the city; XII, 250, of the
Furies sent to destroy Turnus, and elsewhere. These instances
suggest how our term 'apparition' comes to its meaning. Here
Virgil puts the verb in the emphatic place merely to call
attention to the clearness of the atmosphere which allows every
movement of the two birds to be followed. 'Clearly visible
soaring in the transparent air is Nisus.' Note the difference of
force between *apparere* 'to be clearly seen' or conspicuous (see
n. on l. 483) and *videri* 'to appear.' Cf. also its pointed effect
at Lucr. III, 30, quoted on *G.* II, 492. *Apparet* is one of the
specially 'Virgilian' words though used here in its normal
meaning.

405. **Scylla** was daughter of Nisus, King of Megara, which
city Minos was besieging. The life of Nisus depends on a
purple lock of hair which Scylla, who is in love with Minos,
cuts off. Nisus is turned into a sea-eagle and Scylla into
another sea-bird, called *ciris*. This legend forms the subject
of a poem, the *Ciris*, which used to be assigned to Virgil but is
now attributed to Gallus. The last four lines of this poem are
identical with lines 406–9 here. Mackail considers that the
Ciris is in the main the work of Gallus but that the phrases and
passages common to it with the *Georgics* and *Aeneid* were
taken by V. from the *Ciris* and not by the author of *Ciris*
from Virgil. The two young poets worked together and V. may
have contributed lines to his friend's poem. (See Introduction, II.)

406–8. The repetition is meant to suggest the relentlessness
of the pursuit. P. says: "The intention is to emphasize the
ceaseless alternation of flight and pursuit as the eagle keeps
striking and the ciris darting away." The repetition of *pennis*,

auras, auras, pennis, in the concluding words is meant to produce the same effect.

408. **qua se fert Nisus ad auras**. According to K. the eagle, having missed his swoop, has to rise before making another.

410. **liquidas**, 'soft,' 'clear': **presso gutture** is the opposite of *plena voce*, l. 388. "V.'s *corvus* is our old friend the rook, even if some Latin authors use the word equally for rook, crow and raven." The *corvus* since V. describes it here as gregarious cannot mean either the crow or the raven which are not of social habits. *A Year with the Birds*, pp. 233–6.

411. **cubilibus**. Aratus speaks of these softer notes as uttered before the birds go to rest; *cubilibus* may be meant to suggest evening as the time.

412. **nescio...laeti**, 'moved by some mysterious delight': **strepitant**, 'keep up a chattering together.'

413. **iuvat**, emphatic. 'What a joy it is to see again,' explaining *laeti*.

415–16. **sit**, used of a reason not accepted by the speaker as the actual one (Madvig, 357 *b*). V. here explains the weather-instinct of the birds quite as an Epicurean would have done; their physical organisation responds to gradual changes in the atmosphere far more swiftly than ours does. They are not wiser than we. **major** qualifies *prudentia*, not, I think, *ingenium*: 'not that Heaven has granted them wit like ours, or fate any deeper insight into nature.' Lucr. takes the same view as V. on this point: cf. v. 1056–90 which should be read along with this passage: animals, he says, give different cries, according as they are in fear, pain or joy. Crows and rooks "change together with the weather their harsh croakings." C. thinks that V. is referring in *divinitus* and *fato* to two opposite explanations, Platonic or Stoic and materialistic.

418. **vias**, 'modes of action': **uvidus** properly of *Austris*.

420. 'The phases of their minds undergo a change'; **species** is a Lucretian term, slightly modified. Munro defines the meaning in Lucr. as 'the outward form and aspect of anything' as it appears to the eye: sometimes it denotes our power of sight. V. seems to mean by it 'conditions' or 'phases.' Lucr. often insists that 'the nature of mind and soul is bodily'; thus, however ethereal the soul's particles, it must, being corporeal, have a species, a 'form' or 'appearance' of its own which is bound to be affected by changes in its environment.

421. **alios, alios**. The expression is too condensed: 'some movements now, others when the wind, etc.'

422–3 make it clear that V.'s point is the change from low to high spirits. Thus as C. says "the second *alios* is virtually *quam*"; *mutus* is again an Epicurean term: our emotions depend on movements of the soul-atoms.

The young student should note C.'s rendering, 'There lies the secret of the birds' rural chorus, and the ecstasy of the cattle, and the rooks' triumphant paean.'

461–497

461. 'Finally whatever event the fall of evening brings with it, the quarter whence comes the wind that drives away the clouds and leaves the heaven clear, what mischief the rainy South wind is plotting, of all these the Sun will give you warnings.' *Nescis quid vesper serus vehat* was a Roman proverb and was the title of one of Varro's 'Satirae.' 'No one knows what will happen ere fall of night.' **unde serenas...nubes**, lit. 'whence the wind is driving away clear clouds.' Here we have a notable instance of what grammarians call 'proleptic (i.e. anticipatory) expression.' *Serenas* expresses the result of *agat*: the banished clouds leave the sky clear. *Serenas* implies a noun like *caelo* and qualifies it by a Transference of Epithet. Compare *G.* II, 246 of those who taste brackish water, *ora tristia tentantum torquebit*, 'it will twist their mouths and turn them awry.' A notable instance in English poetry occurs in Keats's *Pot of Basil* where Isabella's two brothers, intending to murder her lover in the wood, ride off along with him,

> So the two brothers and their murdered man
> Rode past fair Florence.

As Lewis Campbell says, the effect of such expression is "to present in a single moment what would seem more languid if expanded in the order of time" (Sophocles: second edition, vol. I, p. 70).

P. renders *nubes serenas* 'sunny clouds' adding "the word *nubes* does not necessarily mean a dark cloud," and compares Hor. *Od.* I, 32 where it is used of a cloud round Apollo. But the phrase 'to bring sunny clouds' is very far-fetched in the sense 'to bring fair weather.' N. would render the phrase 'dry' or 'rainless' clouds and quotes *G.* III, 197, *arida nubila*. But *arida* conjoined with *nubila* in this sense is far less strained than *serenas* would be in the same meaning.

464. **etiam**, 'even.' 'Nay, it is he who often gives warning that secret rebellion is imminent.' **tumultus** is used, in a specially Roman sense, of war in Italy. "Our ancestors,"

Cicero says, "spoke of a *tumultus* in Italy because it was a civil war; of a *tumultus* in Gaul because it was on the border of Italy, but they named no other war a *tumultus*," *Phil.* VIII, 1. Thus men used to speak of 'a rising' in our own Highlands. *Tumultus* carried to Roman ears a sense of immediate national danger. P. says: "It is clear from the words *caecos tumultus, fraudem* and *operta bella* that V.'s thoughts are not fixed on the danger of open wars against foreign foes, but on the possibility of secret conspiracies against the power of Augustus, which might end in civil strife, such as in the preceding fifty years had devastated Italy."

465. **fraudem**, 'treason.' **tumescere**, 'were beginning to heave.' A metaphor from the waves rising.

466. Caesar was assassinated on the Ides of March, B.C. 44. According to Servius there was an eclipse of the sun in November of that year. Haverfield says: "Some astronomical calculations made for me show that no solar eclipse was visible in Italy in B.C. 44, and the same conclusion is reached by Hofmann in a tract on ancient eclipses (1884)." But apart from this the atmospheric conditions of that tragic year were very unusual, as we learn from Ovid, Lucan, Plutarch and others. Doubtless the volcanic eruptions referred to by V. and occurring both in Italy and Sicily explain these in part. Keightley reminds us how after the great eruption and earthquake in Calabria, in 1783, the atmosphere of the whole of Europe was during that year more or less obscured.

467. 'In lurid gloom.' **ferrugo**, acc. to Servius a somewhat dark purple: the general meaning is 'dark.' It is sometimes associated with the supernatural: it is the colour of Charon's boat in *Aen.* VI, of Pluto's steeds when he carries off Proserpina (Ovid, *Fasti*), here of the sun's colour under eclipse.

468. 'The godless (or 'unnatural') generation.' Note the order of words in this line, namely two adjectives, verb and two nouns, agreeing with the first and second adjectives and in the same order as the adjectives. Line 497 is exactly similar. Dryden refers to this form of verse as "that which they call golden, or two substantives and two adjectives with a verb between them to keep the peace."

469. **quamquam**, 'yet it was not the sun alone that gave portents.'

470. **obscenae**, 'ill-omened,' **importunae**, 'with boding voice.' C. says 'virtually synonymous with *obscenae*,' itself repeatedly coupled with *volucres* in the *Aen.* (But see Fowler, *Death of Turnus*, p. 151.) Acc. to Servius, *importunae* is='unseason-

able,' as of nocturnal birds appearing in the day-time. Cf. Shakespeare, *Jul. Caesar*, 1, 3,

> And yesterday'the bird of night did sit
> Even at noonday, upon the market-place,
> Hooting and shrieking.

471. **signa dabant** seems to imply that these portents were forewarnings of Caesar's death, but they are recorded by Dio and others as following it. See n. on l. 489. Cicero again in his Fourth Philippic, c. 4, delivered in Dec. 44, treats them as foretelling punishment speedily to fall upon Antony. Servius quotes from Livy to the effect that a tremendous eruption of Aetna occurred 'before Caesar's death.'

472. **Aetnam undantem**, 'the lava-stream from Aetna.'

473. **volvere**, 'sent whirling through the air.'

474-6. 'A voice was heard far and wide through the silent groves, a mighty voice.' The pause after a spondaic first foot in 477 suggests the awe of the supernatural. C. compares the voice heard in the temple, just before the taking of Jerusalem, 'Let us depart hence.' **Germania** probably refers to Roman legions on the Rhine. "Caesar made two short raids across the Rhine, but Rome got no footing in Germany till after Caesar's death," S.

477. The words **simulacra...miris** are borrowed from Lucr. 1, 123.

479. **terrae**. "The plural implies that there were numerous or repeated earthquakes," C.

482. **fluviorum**, here three long syllables. The short *u* of *flŭvius* is here lengthened because followed by two spirants *u* and *i* which have here the force of consonants: so at l. 397 *tĕnuia* is scanned as a dactyl; so also *ăriete*, *păriete*.

483. We must supplement the literal sense a little in rendering *eodem*. 'Nor in that terrible time was there any respite either in the threatening filaments that stood out on the ill-boding entrails or in the flow of blood from the wells.' Note the force of *appareo*.

484. **fibrae**, probably veins or markings on the liver of the victim when examined by the augur.

488. **diri**, 'appalling.'

489. **ergo**. These portents did not merely foreshadow disaster but retribution in the form of civil war for Caesar's murder. **paribus telis**, 'armed alike,' as Lucan says, *Obvia signis Signa pares aquilas et pila minantia pilis*; the *pilum* was a characteristic Roman weapon.

491. 'Nor did it seem to the gods undeserved.' **superis,**

an ethical dative acc. to C. who quotes Lucan x, 102 *sat fuit indignum, Caesar, mundoque tibique.*

The great battle of Pharsalia in which Caesar crushed Pompey and ended the Civil War was fought in Thessaly in B.C. 48, and Philippi in the same region in B.C. 42, when Octavian and Antony defeated Brutus and Cassius, the murderers of Julius Caesar. Both sites, though many miles from each other, were in the Roman province of Macedonia. iterum (490) must be taken with *concurrere* not with *videre,* which last would imply that Pharsalia and Philippi were on the same spot. But V.'s geography in 491–2 is very vague. **Emathia** was a part of Macedonia while **Haemus,** now called the Balkan, is far distant from Philippi.

493. **scilicet** introduces a strong asseveration, 'Yes, and the time will come.'

494. **molitus,** 'when he heaves up the ground.' See note on 329.

497. **grandia ossa,** 'the huge bones.' It is not necessary to read here an adoption of Lucretius' view that the earth is growing old and near its end. It was generally believed that the human race was becoming enfeebled and each generation of men smaller than the last. Thus Aeneas in *Aen.* XII, 899 hurls a mighty stone at Turnus: 'scarce could twelve picked men lift it, such puny frames as earth now-a-days produces.'

498–514

498. **Indigetes,** 'native powers,' i.e. heroes of Rome like Aeneas and Romulus who had been deified. Thus Vesta was one of the *Di patrii* and Romulus one of the *Indigetes.* The word is derived from *indu,* 'within' and the root of *gigno.*

499. Romulus was believed to have founded Rome on the Palatine and here too was the palace of Augustus.

500. **hunc saltem,** 'this youth at least,' since Julius Caesar had been cut off so prematurely. Augustus was at this time about 28 years old. The term *iuvenis* makes a pathetic appeal to Heaven. **iuvenem.** Haverfield's note on the term is very interesting: "Augustus was only nineteen when he began his career in 44 B.C., as he observes himself (see sec. 1 of the Monumentum Ancyranum, an inscription recording his own career which Augustus had set up in various cities of the Empire), and his youth is emphasized by Cicero (*adulescens vel puer potius,* etc.) and Virgil, *E.* I, 43, writing not long after. Later writers continue the idea, as Virgil here, Horace, *Od.* I, 11, 41 (probably B.C. 29): a hieroglyphic inscription at Philae,

dated B.C. 29, calls him 'the beautiful youth,' and his youthful head appears on his coins after 27 B.C." (See C. 5th ed. 1898.) It is plain that the term was welcome to Augustus.

502. **luimus**, present tense. Here and elsewhere V. lays stress upon the old legend that Laomedon, King of Troy, had made a contract with Poseidon (Neptune) and Apollo to build walls for his city, but after the walls were built refused to pay the price. Greek religion included, as the Greek drama shows, a strong belief that the sins of the parents are visited on the children. Thus Rome is conceived by V. to inherit the guilt and still to be paying the penalty for its remote ancestor's crime. So the Harpy taunts the Trojans with being Laomedontiadae, 'true sons of Laomedon,' *Aen.* III, 248, cf. IV, 542 *Laomedonteae periuria gentis*, V, 811 *periurae moenia Troiae*.

505. **quippe** gives the reason why, 'Heaven has long grudged Augustus to earth.' V. strikes again the same unworthy note of adulation as in the opening of the poem. **ubi** = *apud quos* (*homines*, l. 504), 'since among men right and wrong are confounded,' lit. 'inverted'; good seems evil and evil good in their eyes. P. very properly calls attention to the confusion of all moral sense in Greece during the Peloponnesian War as described by Thucydides III, 82. Greece was, however, at no time a united nation such as Italy had been, and Greeks could not regard the Peloponnesian War as a crime, in the way that Romans regarded their own civil wars.

506. **aratro**, probably dative, 'the plough is not given its due honour.'

507. 'The husbandmen have been marched away and the fields are thick with weeds.'

509–11. It is difficult to fix the exact date of the wars referred to. **vicinae urbes.** Some cities in Italy especially in Etruria took sides with Antony and were not easily subdued. The **Mars impius**, 'unholy Civil War,' refers to the struggle between Antony and Octavian which was decided at Actium in 31 B.C.

510. **ruptis legibus inter se**, 'breaking their mutual league.' Neighbouring cities in Italy, especially in Etruria, took opposite sides in the Civil Wars. Euphrates refers to the war with Parthia, where Antony was in command.

511. **arma ferunt**, 'are up in arms.' **impius** in Latin carries a special condemnation, as denoting what is 'unnatural' as well as 'unholy.' *pietas* expresses both natural affection to parents, duty to one's country, and obedience to the known will of the gods. *Impius*, says Dr W. Fowler, "expresses the nearest

approach in Roman antiquity to our idea of sin" (*R.E.R.* p. 462).

512. **carceres** were stalls at the end of the circus with gates, which were opened simultaneously to allow the chariots to start.

513. **addunt in spatia**. *Addunt* is either used absolutely, of which there is no other instance, or *se* may be supplied from *effudere*. We find *addere gradum* in the sense of 'to go quicker' Liv. III, 27. The Berne Scholiast calls *addunt* "propria vox circi." In a technical term of the race-course *gradum* might be dropped. **spatia** denotes the 'laps' or rounds of the circus, which the chariots had to complete; *in spatia* would then mean 'over the course,' lit. 'from lap to lap,' like *in dies, in annos*.

513-14. **tendens**, 'straining at the reins.' **currus** used for 'the team' here and at *G.* III, 91 and IV, 389. **fertur**, 'is carried away.' **auriga**, "Servius suggests that the charioteer hurried on by furious horses is Octavian, but this hardly agrees with l. 500," C.

In this concluding passage V. expresses the feeling of the men of his time that Rome was now paying retribution for the crime of her foremost citizens, who had so recklessly sacrificed their country to their own private ambition. See Introduction, § 1. Nettleship says: "The end of the first *Georgic* is best referred to the period immediately preceding the civil war which ended at Actium. Octavianus is not spoken of as victorious but prayed for as the only hope of his falling country." *Ancient Lives of Vergil*, p. 57.

GEORGIC II

1–8

Ll. 1–8 describe the subjects of the second *Georgic*, namely the culture of the olive and other fruit-trees but especially of the vine.

1. **hactenus** sc. *cecini*. **sidera caeli**, because these fix the time for sowing different crops.

2, 3. **silvestria virgulta**, 'the young trees of the forest.' *Virgultum* denotes a collection of trees, low or young, 'a copse,' brushwood. **Bacche...tecum**, because such young trees were used as supports for the vine.. **prolem**, because he is to treat of the propagation of olive trees. **tarde crescentis**, Hesiod quoted by Pliny xv, 1, says that the planter (or possibly 'the sower,' *sator*) of an olive rarely saw its fruit.

4. **huc**, i.e. *veni* from l. 7. 'Come, in order to inspire me.' **Lenaee**, a Greek title of Bacchus (Gk. *lenos*, 'a wine-press').

5, 6. **gravidus**. When a short final syllable is made emphatic by the ictus falling upon it, V. occasionally lengthens it: see n. on 1, 138. **tibi** taken with *floret*, 'for thee (as giver of increase) 'the vineyard looks bright, teeming with rich clusters,' cf. *cui* in *G.* 1, 14 and in the invocation to Venus (Lucr. 1, 7) *tibi suavis daedala tellus summittit flores*. **floreo**, 'to blossom,' is used of things that display the beauty of their prime. Cf. its use in Lucr. quoted on l. 327.

8. **tinguo** means either 'to plunge' or 'to stain.' **mecum**. V. seems to identify himself with the husbandman.

35–82

35. 'The culture proper to each tree after its kind.' **generatim**, a Lucretian word.

36. **mollire**, 'to mellow.'

37. **iuvat**, 'what joy to plant,' C. V. means not merely, as K. puts it, that mountains may be made productive but that here is a triumph of man over nature. **Ismarus** and **Taburnus** were mountains, the former, famous for its vines, in Thrace, the latter, famous for olives, in Samnium close to the Caudine Pass.

39. **decurre**, a metaphor from ships, *decurro* is used of sailing to the land from the high seas, as at *Aen.* v, 212; so here it means to run over the whole course to the end: *laborem* is a cognate accusative.

40. 'Thou, who dost well deserve the largest share of my fame,' because V. undertook the task at Maecenas' request.

42-4. **non...ferrea vox**, an imitation of Homer, *Il.* ii, 488-490; *non* in l. 43 of course implies *optem* as apodosis to *si sint.*

41. **pelago**, 'ocean' not 'sea.'

44. **primi litoris oram** = *primam litoris oram.* The metaphor seems to jar with l. 41 when he invites Maecenas to sail with him over a vast ocean. But lest this should alarm Maecenas, he continues modestly that he cannot deal with it fully but will only 'coast the very edge of the shore.'

45. 'At this point of my narrative I shall not detain you with romantic fictions, told in circuitous detail with long preludes.' **carmine ficto** refers to the legends of mythology, which furnished the well-worn subject of the average poet of V.'s day. In the opening of *G.* iii he again refuses to deal with this. Myers suggests (*Classical Essays*, p. 153) that these lines imply an apology for the introduction to *G.* i, with its conventional and frigid mythology. If this be so, it is a sign of the growth which marks V.'s whole career as a poet, ever in increasing touch with reality. See note before *G.* iii.

47. **tollunt se**, 'rear themselves up to the shores of light.' **luminis oras**, a favourite and majestic phrase of Lucr. "He seems to denote by it the line or border, which divides light from darkness, being from non-being, for he almost always uses *orae* in its proper sense, that of an edge or coast or limiting line" (Munro on 1, 22). The phrase is found twice in Ennius. In Lucr.'s poem *luminis orae* means the realm of living things; at 1, 22, in despite of his philosophy he qualifies *oras* by the term *dias*, 'divine.' It is most properly used of the birth of a child, or as here of a plant springing out of the ground.

48. **laeta**, 'luxuriant.'

49. **quippe solo natura subest**, 'since productive power is latent in the soil.' The wording seems to echo Lucr. Lucr. uses the word *subest* to describe the fourth element of the soul, secreted deep within it, which is its most vital part, being to the soul what the soul is to the body. *Nam penitus prorsum Latet haec natura subestque*, Lucr. iii, 273. Munro says: "Perhaps every one of the many meanings which *natura* has in Cicero or 'nature' in English is found in Lucr. Sometimes it is an active force or agency, sometimes an inert mass, some-

times an abstract term, sometimes as at 1, 419 it seems synonymous with the *omne*, 'the universe'" (Note on Lucr. 1, 25).

50. **si quis inserat**, 'if any one were to graft cuttings on these or to commit them when transplanted to well-dug trenches, they would throw off their wild character, and under steady cultivation will follow you to whatever qualities you may invite them.'

51-2. **exuerint, sequentur.** The indicatives instead of the normal subjunctive here represent "a change for the sake of vividness: the condition supposed to be realised and the consequences then will (not would) follow. So with pathetic force *Aen.* VI, 882 *si qua fata aspera rumpas tu Marcellus eris,*" S. The Medicean MS. has *voles.*

51. **exuerint**, 'they are likely to throw off.' The emendation *voles* is not necessary: *sequentur* very naturally follows *voces,* which last may be explained as the indefinite use of the second person of the subjunctive, 'one' or 'some one' (Madvig, *Lat. Gr.* § 370). Several Roman writers on agriculture say that mere transplanting will improve a tree.

52. **artes** means any qualities acquired by training as opposed to natural ones.

54. 'If it be planted out in the open fields,' i.e. removed from the wood, with room to grow in.

56. 'And wither up its power to bear.'

57. **iam**, almost = *praeterea*, introducing a fresh point, 'again'; **seminibus iactis**, 'chance dropped seeds.'

58. 'For generations yet unborn,' C.

59. **poma**, 'fruit' in general, including all except grapes, nuts and, according to some, figs (C. on *Ecl.* II, 53).

60. Strictly the *racemi* were minor clusters of the bunch of grapes.

61. **scilicet**, 'the fact is, all must be forced into the trench (when they are planted) and broken in at great cost of toil.'

64. **respondent**, 'answer best from truncheons,' i.e. pieces of the trunk planted, see l. 24. **Paphiae** from Paphos in Cyprus, famous for its temple of Venus. For the epithet see on *G.* I, 120.

66. **arbos.** This was the poplar.

69. 'Is grafted with the fruit of the walnut.' Note the hypermeter. The extra syllable is elided before *et* of 70, but this does not, as a rule, occur unless the final syllable is preceded by a long one. (Keightley adopts the reading found in the Med. as a correction and in other MSS. *inseritur vero et*

nucis arbutus horrida fetu. **horrida**, from the ruggedness of the bark.

70-2. The three verbs are in the 'gnomic' perfect because expressing habitual action. Hence the perfect is used in proverbs (*gnomae*). Acc. to V. the walnut can be grafted on the arbutus, the apple on the plane, the chestnut on the beech, the pear on the 'ornus,' and the oak on the elm. But botanists know that a tree can only be grafted on another of the same family as its own. Therefore such grafts are impossible. Columella, who wrote on agriculture about A.D. 50, says that the old agriculturists maintained that any tree may be grafted upon any other provided that the bark and fruit are not dissimilar.

71. **fagus** with *u* made long by arsis. Nearly all MSS. have *fagos*, evidently a correction for the sake of the metre. But no one would graft a beech on a valuable chestnut.

73. **modus inserere** = *modus inserendi*, the genitive being explanatory, cf. *G.* i, 305 *tempus stringere glandes.* See Madvig, § 417. **simplex** = *unus*, 'one and the same.' So *simplex*, 'one single' at Lucr. v, 613 and 620.

75. **tenues tunicas**, 'their delicate sheaths,' namely the inner bark under the cortex. 'A narrow slit is made in the knot thus formed' by the sprouting bud. **aliena ex arbore**, 'from a strange tree.'

77. **udo libro**, 'into the sap-full bark,' *udo*, lit. 'moist,' with the sap which is the life of the tree. 'Or again the trunks are cut back, when they are knotless and a passage is cleft into the solid wood.'

80-1. **plantae**, 'shoots.' **exiit**, the perfect here expresses suddenness, 'and lo! a huge tree has shot up.' Note the use of *et* which C. calls 'a remnant of primitive simplicity of expression,' such co-ordination of clauses being more forcible than the use of a conjunction like *cum*. He compares *Aen.* III, 9 *vix prima inceperat aestas Et pater Anchises dare fatis vela iubebat.* The Roman husbandman followed methods of grafting which are fully described by Cato and Columella. The first which is now called inoculation or budding was to select a healthy bud and remove it along with two square inches of the bark surrounding it. They then removed an equal extent of bark from the tree to be grafted and put in its place the bark containing the bud, making the edges of both meet close. They then bound up the whole, leaving the bud free and covered the binding with moist clay. The second method was to saw off the head of the trunk of the tree to be grafted. They next inserted the shoot in its place, repeating the operation as desired. See other methods under *Inoculatio* in Keightley's *Terms of Husbandry*.

The instances given by V. in ll. 69–72 are merely speculative. Actual experience would at once have checked such wild experimenting. In V.'s day grafting was probably confined to implanting a shoot from a cultivated tree on a wild stock of the same kind, e.g. the garden olive on the oleaster or the apple on the crab.

109–122, 136–176

111. The **ornus** used to be identified with the Mountain Ash or Rowan, but this with its abundant red berries could hardly be called *sterilis*: botanists are now inclined to think it the Manna Ash of Calabria.

112. 'Myrtle thickets grow most luxuriantly on the seashore.' **laetus** is generally applied to crops but here to the ground.

114. **extremis**, evidently a transference of epithet for *extremum orbem*, 'look also at the ends of the earth where it has been subdued by tillage.' **cultoribus**, dative of the agent, found after passive participles, as at *Aen.* IX, 565 *agnum quaesitum matri*; VI, 509 *nihil tibi relictum*, 'nothing has been left undone by thee.'

115. **pictos**, 'tattooed.' **Geloni**, a Scythian tribe in the Ukraine.

116. Lit. 'their native countries have been divided among trees,' i.e. 'each tree has its allotted country.'

117. **Sabaeis**. The Arabs of Sheba in Arabia Felix, cf. 1 Kings x. 10, where the Queen of Sheba gives Solomon 'of spice very great store.'

119. **acanthus**, not here the graceful-leaved herb, Brank-Ursine, named by V. at *G.* IV, 123, which is said to have furnished the idea of the Corinthian capital, but a tree, the Acacia, which yields gum-arabic and also balsam, the Balm of Gilead, found in Arabia and Palestine. (The tree, however, bears pods and not berries.) Both the herb in its wild state and the tree have prickles or thorns. See Keightley's *Flora Virgiliana*.

120. **lana**, 'cotton,' which is cultivated in Greece, Malta and Sicily. It is the produce of two kinds of Gossypium; Herodotus calls it 'wool off a tree.'

121. **Seres**. This name included the Chinese, and silken garments were called *serica*. V. means that silk, like cotton,

is a vegetable product combed from the leaves of trees. This was the common opinion of the ancients. Pliny (VI, 17) says that, when the thick silken cloths of the East were brought to Europe, the threads composing them were untwisted and the silk woven again into thinner webs. Ammianus however (XXIII, 6, who wrote about A.D. 400) hints at the process of dipping the cocoons into warm water in order to wind off the silk. Aristotle (*H.A.* v, 19) tells us that silk was obtained from some insect and was first woven by a woman of the island of Cos in the Aegean named Pamphile. Pausanias (VI, 26) says that the threads of which the Seres made garments were formed by a little animal resembling a spider which they kept in boxes and fed during winter and summer. The knowledge of mulberry-leaves being the proper food of the silkworm was not brought to Constantinople till about A.D. 520. See K. pp. 368–70 and also the very interesting note in the translation of Pausanias by Frazer, who says "Pausanias appears to have been the first ancient writer who calls the silk-worm by its Chinese name *Ser* (in Korean *Sir*)."

136–176 is a panegyric on Italy. Sellar writes: "In this episode the sorrow for the past and foreboding for the future which marks the close of the first book of the *Georgics*, has entirely cleared away. The feeling now expressed is one of pride and exultation in Italy.

> extulit haec Decios, Marios, magnosque Camillos,
> Scipiadas duros bello, et te, maxime Caesar.

This passage is a counter-picture to that of the rank luxuriance of Nature in the vast forests and jungles of the East," Chap. VI, 4. V.'s country is the inspiration of his poem, 'Hail to thee,' he says, 'O land of Saturn, mighty mother of noble fruits and noble men; 'Tis for thee that I essay the theme of the glory, and the skill (in agriculture) of olden days.'

136. **silvae** might be gen. after *ditissima*. Manilius, who imitates the line at IV, 472 evidently took it thus. But probably C. is right in retaining the old interpretation making *terra* in apposition to *Medorum silvae*.

137. **Hermus**, a river of Lydia. **auro turbidus**, 'whose mud (or sand) is gold.'

138. **certent** is evidently potential, 'could vie.'

139. Euhemeros, a Sicilian, about 316 B.C. being furnished by the king of Macedonia with money, went a long journey of which he wrote a narrative. "His name has become connected with his method of treating the legends of Gods and

heroes as exaggerated records of ordinary men. He tells of an island, Panchaia near Arabia, very rich and happy. V. uses the name here as we might speak of Eldorado," S. **Panchaia**, four syllables here.

141. **satis...hydri** might be effectively rendered as a parallel clause. 'Here is a land where no bulls, etc., a land where no huge dragon's teeth were ever sown.'

143. **humor**, 'the juice.' The famous Falernian wine grew at the foot of Mount Massicus in Campania.

144. **laeta**, 'prolific.'

145. 'Hence comes the war-horse that prances proudly over the battlefield.'

146. **Clitumnus**, a river of Umbria. The oxen of the district were famous for their pure whiteness, supposed to be derived from the water of the river. Such milk-white bulls were chosen for sacrifice on the occasion of a triumph and were led before the victor's car to the Capitol (*templa*).

149. 'Everlasting spring and summer in months which are not summer-time' as if Italy had no seasons but spring and summer. The expression *alienis mensibus* seems suggested by Lucr. 1, 181 *alienis partibus anni*, of plants coming up out of their proper season. V.'s instances here seem to contradict Lucr.'s reasoning at 1, 159–214. If there were no atoms, no fixed base of things, there would be no constancy in nature: any tree might produce any fruit, any animal beget any other. The rose or corn or grapes would not be produced at fixed seasons but each at any period of the year, *incerto spatio atque alienis partibus anni*, ll. 180–1.

150. **bis**, 'twice in the year.' **pomis**, probably dative, 'serviceable for fruit,' so C. According to Varro (*R.R.* 1, 7) in the district of Consentia in Bruttium the apple-trees bore fruit twice a year.

152. But according to Dioscorides the Aconite or Monks-hood grows abundantly in a district of the Apennines. Servius also asserts it to grow in Italy. But the term may include other poisonous plants.

153–4. The emphasis of position and meaning lies on *immensos* and *tanto*. V. cannot mean there are no snakes but simply none so huge as elsewhere. **rapit**, of hasty motion 'darts.' **neque tanto**, 'nor does he coil himself into a spire with so vast a train as in other lands.' "The striking pause after *humum* contrasts the serpent's stoppage 'as it gathers itself into a spire' with its previous smooth and rapid movement," P.

155. **adde,** 'remember too.' **operumque laborem,** 'and triumphs of human toil.'

156. **congesta,** 'piled up.' Many of the ancient Italian towns were thus built on steep heights. The picture given in these two lines could hardly be more perfect. The contrast between the toilsome feat of building on such precipitous spots and the streams gliding peacefully below the time-hallowed walls, as Sellar says, emphasizes the features of the great Italian towns so that these lines 'recur to every traveller as he passes through Italy.'

158. The two seas are the Mare Superum or Adriatic and the Mare Inferum or Tyrrhene sea, that between Italy and Sicily.

159. **Larius** (sc. *lacus*), lake of Como; Benacus, lake of Garda.

160. **marino,** 'like the ocean.'

161–4. These lines refer to the Portus Julius, a fine harbour made by Agrippa under the orders of Augustus in 37 B.C. Not far from Naples were two small lakes close to the sea, Lucrinus and Avernus, the latter in an extinct volcanic crater. The two lakes were joined and the barrier between Lucrinus and the sea was strengthened by a breakwater (*claustra*) through which a passage was cut, large enough to admit ships. The breakwater kept the sea from damaging the harbour while the passage allowed its waters to enter the lake.

162. 'The rage and loud thunder of the baffled waters,' C. **aequor** and **pontus** refer to the same thing. Keightley says: "The meaning of this seems to be that the sea rushed against and was flung back (*refuso*) by the dyke and that the sound was heard all over the new-formed harbour."

164. **Avernis.** "A contrast seems intended between Tyrrhenus and Avernus," says C., the sea-water passing through the Lucrine into the Avernus, which was the inner of the two lakes.

165. **haec eadem,** 'it is a land too which has disclosed from her veins streams of silver...and has flowed with abundance of gold.' In reality Italy is by no means rich in minerals. The reference is probably to lodes of metal. Gold was found in the Po according to Pliny, XXXII, 4. He also tells us that the Senate forbade the working of mines in Italy probably in order to check wasteful speculations. "The perfects *ostendit* and *fluxit* may point to the discontinuance of working the mines, though they need only mean 'it has been known to display, etc.'" C.

167. **acre,** 'spirited.'

168. **malo,** 'hardships.' **verutos,** 'armed with the verutum' for which the term *veru* is used in poetry. This was a short pike used by the Volsci and Sabines and adopted by the Roman light infantry. The Marsians lived in the hill-country, some 50 miles east from Rome, and the Sabines in the hills to the north-east. Both races were famous for their bravery and took an active part against Rome in the Social War.

169. **Decios,** etc. The plural here is used generically to denote a type even though only one person is meant as in the case of Marius and Camillus. So we might speak of 'Britain's Wellingtons' or 'a Wellington,' 'a Nelson.' Two Decii, father and son, devoted themselves to death in the solemn form, acc. to which a Roman commander was believed to secure victory for his country, the father in the war with the Latins in 340 B.C. and the son at Sentinum against the Gauls.

170. **Scipiadas,** the form *Scipiones* is impossible in hexa-meter verse; the Homeric patronymic is strangely blended with the Roman name, cf. Memmiadae in Lucr. 1, 26. P. Cornelius Scipio Africanus Major defeated Hannibal finally at Zama in Africa 202 B.C. and P. Corn. Scip. Aemilianus Africanus Minor took Carthage 146 B.C. and made Africa a Roman province. Camillus saved Rome from the Gauls 390 B.C. and Marius saved her from the Teutons and Cimbri in 102 and 101 B.C. These were the proudest names on Rome's roll of fame.

171-2. **nunc iam victor,** 'at this time already victorious.' This refers to the battle of Actium, 31 B.C. **inbellem Indum.** The latter word is used to include any Oriental people. By this epithet V. means nothing less than to depreciate the victory of Augustus. *imbellem* emphasises the Roman self-respect and the animosity and indignation of the true Romans against 'the attempt of Antony to set up a rival Oriental dominion and the rescue of Romanism and civilisation by Augustus.' It also expresses the Roman contempt for the despotic rulers and consequent degradation of the East. See Warde Fowler's Chapter on V. *R.E.R.* After Actium Augustus made a triumphant progress through Syria, Palestine and Asia Minor, and the Eastern peoples generally sought to make peace with him. **Romanis arcibus,** 'the seven hills of Rome' as at l. 535. These lines are thought to have been inserted after the com-pletion of the *Georgics*.

174. **tibi** not *ingredior* is emphatic. V. has by this time made good way in his subject. 'It is in thy honour that I essay the theme of the glory and skill in husbandry of olden days.'

175. **recludere,** 'to unseal' the holy fountains. Cf. Lucretius

I, 927, *iuvat integros accedere fontis atque haurire*, 'it delights me to approach the untasted springs and drink,' because, he explains, his aim is to deliver men from slavery to religion, but the metaphor of 'the holy fount' in V. along with *ausus* claims not only the daring of being the first to attempt in Latin a poem on agriculture but also carries with it a religious notion—'He is the first that has been thought worthy to unseal the holy spring,' C. Cf. l. 476.

176. **Ascra**, near Helicon in Northern Greece, was the birth-place of Hesiod, whose poem *The Works and Days* was the first of which agriculture was the subject.

315–345

315. **tam prudens**, 'nor let any adviser have such credit for foresight ('how wise soever' Mackail) as to persuade you,' C.

316. **rigidam**, 'when it is lying stiff.'

317. **semine iacto**, 'when the young shoots are set': l. 318 shows that V. refers to vines: *semen* has the same sense at l. 302 *neu ferro laede retunso semina*, and 268. P. well compares the use of *iacere* with *fundamenta*, which is found in Cicero and Livy.

318. 'Nor does it suffer the young plant to attach its frozen root to the soil.' C. prefers to take **concretam**=*ita ut concrescat*, sc. *terrae*.

319. **rubenti**, literally 'glowing,' 'in the bloom of spring.' Cf. *G.* IV, 306 *ante novis rubeant quam prata coloribus*.

320. **avis** is the stork.

321. **rapidus Sol**, 'the fiery Sun.' Keightley (Excursus II) has shown that adjectives in *-idus* have a participial force, so that *rapidus* is nearly equivalent to *rapiens* and *rapax* and appears to signify 'carrying away' and hence 'consuming.' C. too accepts this view, saying "*rapidus* in the original sense seems to be nearly a synonym of *rapax*. Hence the word is applied to devouring seas and fire and to the scorching sun." (On *Ecl.* II, 10.)

323. **adeo** lays stress on *ver*. 'Spring it is, Spring that does good to the leafage of the woodlands and the forests.' K. explains **nemorum** as 'plantations,' the trees in the *arbustum* which were planted in regular rows and on which the vines were to be trained. "The *arbustum* is opposed to the *vinea* in which they were trained on espaliers from 4 to 7 feet high and stood without support or were left to run along the ground," K. (*Terms of Husbandry*).

324. **genitalia**, 'vitalising.'

326. 'And, blending in his might with her mighty frame, nourishes all her growth.'

327. **alit**, V. departs from his metaphor simply to say that rain is essential to growth. Here, as so often in the second *Georgic*, V. is inspired by Lucretius. Cf. the lines (*De Rerum Natura* I, 250) *postremo pereunt imbres, ubi eos pater Aether In gremium matris terrai praecipitavit; At nitidae surgunt fruges ramique virescunt Arboribus...Hinc laetas urbes pueris florere videmus Frondiferasque novis avibus canere undique silvas.* But the last two lines have a touch which is not Virgilian; the streets 'blossoming with children' and 'the leafy forests ringing (lit. singing) on all sides with new birds' stand out clear before us under the spring sunshine as if called up by magic.

329. **Venerem repetunt**, 'pair.'

331. **laxant sinus**, 'the fields open their bosoms to the warm breezes,' continuing the beautiful image at l. 325 of a marriage between Heaven and Earth. 'A soft moisture abounds everywhere.' **omnibus** sc. *arvis*.

332. The suns are new because they are the beginning of the warm season: **soles** are the suns of each day. For *gramina* several MSS. and Celsus read **germina**, which P. and S. adopt. In the sense 'young shoots,' *germina* with the reference to the vine immediately following suits the general meaning of the passage best. Hirzel and C. read *gramina* but the latter accepts it in a very doubtful way: he quotes Horace on the coming of spring: *redeunt iam gramina campis arboribusque comae (Odes* IV, 7).

336. **non alios inluxisse dies**, 'that the days were brighter or their course more blissful,' C. **non alios**. Does this mean 'different from what they were' in V.'s day? and is the poet protesting against Lucr.'s doctrine that the world is growing old,—a doctrine which V. does not accept? Probably not: *non alios* simply enforces the statement—At no other season than spring could the world have come into being.

338. **crediderim**. The perfect subjunctive generally, in the first person, used in modest assertion, 'to my thinking' Mackail. **ver illud erat**, ''twas springtime then.'

340. **lucem hausere**, 'opened their eyes on the light.' *Haurio* is used of drinking in through the eyes and ears as well as through the mouth. In *Ecl.* VI, 33 V. speaks of the ether as *liquidus ignis*.

341. **ferrea**, the reading of almost all the MSS., is followed by

C. and S. Another reading, *terrea*, found as a correction in one good MS. and also in most of the MSS. of Lactantius, affords material for a good-going controversy. *Terrea* which Page and Hirzel accept, might be thought to express Lucretius' strange theory of the origin of mankind by generation from the earth which he supposes to have been full of sap like a mother's milk (v. 806-820). On the other hand *ferrea*, says C., is supported by lines like *lapides...unde homines nati, durum genus*, G. I, 63, 'men are hard because born of the stones,' as well as by Lucr. v, 925 *At genus humanum multo fuit illud in arvis Durius, ut decuit, tellus quod dura creasset*, and is in complete keeping with V.'s dominant feeling, the glorification of labour. The last reason is weighty. Moreover as Papillon says, *terrea* is less forcible and is tautological with *arvis*. Had V. here intended to express Lucr.'s notion of infants being fed from the juices of the earth, he would hardly have used *duris arvis* since at v, 780 Lucr. dwells on the softness of the earth (*mollia terrae arva*). The Iron Age of the myths does not date from so far back as the world's spring-time, nor is V., whose cosmogony is so strange a mixture of Epicureanism and mythology, thinking about any 'Iron Age' here. One dominant thought of the *Georgics* is that men are 'hard,' i.e. to say 'enduring' and strong, which is in keeping with an 'iron race,' but not with the strange Lucretian notion as to the origin of men from the earth. Servius also read *ferrea* which he explains to mean *procreata ex lapidibus ad laborem*. "*ferrea* suggests V.'s constant idea of man born to labour and endurance: he felt deeply both the dignity of labour (the side most prominent in the *Georgics*) and the sadness and suffering of human life. The contrast with the fertility and beauty of the great spring is felt, though, with V.'s usual felicity, it is given in the lightest of touches," Sidgwick.

342. **immissae**, 'were let loose' Mackail. The stars are conceived as living inhabitants of heaven after the Pythagorean notion. Ovid expressly calls them *animantes* (*Met.* I, 73). Even Lucretius cannot escape speaking of the stars as if they were living. See *Lucretius: Epicurean and Poet*, Chap. XIII.

343-5. 'Nor could young creatures endure all the hardship such as frosts, storms, etc. unless there were a great breathing-time like this, coming between the cold and the heat, and a clement sky were waiting to welcome the earth.' **tanta quies** is in contrast to *laborem*. **excipere** means to receive a thing from or after some person or some previous condition (so at Lucr v, 829, which V. may have had in mind here. *accipere hospitio* means 'to welcome a guest after a journey ').

362–370

There are three stages in the growth of the vine, marked by *dum, dum* and *ubi*. It must be left alone in the first, only the leaves thinned by the hand in the second, in the last use the knife freely.

362. 'While the earliest growth is maturing with its first leaves.'

363. **agit se**, 'is pushing its way.'

364. **palmes**, denotes a vine-shoot which has begun to bear grapes. **purum**, if not merely a synonym for *aethera*, must refer, as C. says, to the freedom of the empty sky. So at l. 287 the branches must be given free growing room. Cf. *pura terra*, ground cleared from stones or bushes.

laxis immissus habenis, 'launching out into the air in full career' (*immissus* is deponent here). The expression is certainly suggested by one of Lucretius' most vivid metaphors, how the trees in the first spring-time (as in every spring) vie with each other, 'racing at full gallop,' which shall be first to put forth bud and leaf. *Arboribusque datumst variis exinde per auras Crescendi magnum immissis certamen habenis*, v, 786–7. The metaphor is more in keeping with forest-trees, ash or elm or oak, than with the shooting vine-branches. At the same time, *immitto* has also a special meaning, 'to let anything grow without restraint,' as in Varro, *R.R.* 1, 31, 3 *vitis immittitur ad uvas pariendas*, and *Aen.* III, 593 and elsewhere, *barba immissa*. V. separates *immissus* from *habenis* as in the usual phrase and makes it agree with *palmes*, filling its place by *laxis*. As C. says, "this is acc. to V.'s habit of hinting at one mode of expression while actually using another." This line shows again how saturated was Virgil's mind from youth up with Lucretius' imagery and language, so much so that, as Munro says, "he imitates Lucretius' language and rhythm, while the sense is quite different." See his note on 1, 253. In fact, while we read him, V.'s rhythm keeps constantly calling up Lucretian echoes.

365. **ipsa**, i.e. *vitis* contrasted with *palmes*; **temptanda**, perhaps 'experimented on.'

368. **exierint**, 'have shot up.'

370. **exerce imperia**, 'set up a firm rule.' Cf. 1, 99 of the thorough-going farmer, *imperat arvis*.

458-474

458. **si norint**, 'could they but know.' It corresponds to the present not the imperfect subjunctive: Kennedy says, "this protasis shows that *futuros* is to be supplied with *fortunatos*, 'How blessed are they and will they be if they come to know.'" It must be rendered 'did they but know,' C. This saying embodies much of V.'s philosophy of life. Note the violent opposition between these words and *discordibus armis*, a contrast that came close home to V.'s generation.

460. **fundit** not *fundat*, as C. reminds us, "because the words *quibus—tellus* are part of the subject as well as *agricolae*," the clause being intended to describe the farmer's happiness rather than to give a reason for it. *Fundat* would weaken the assertion. **humo**, 'from her soil.'

462. **mane**. These receptions were held from six in the morning till eight. **vomit totis aedibus**, 'disgorges from all its apartments.'

463. **inhiant**, the nom. being *agricolae*.

464. **inlusas**, 'tricked out,' 'fancifully wrought.' *Ludere* and *lusus* being used of poetry (especially by V.) and music. Here the phrase sounds contemptuous: it suggests labour wasted on anything. **Ephyreia**. The bronzes of Corinth (for which 'Ephyre' was the old Homeric name) were highly valued.

465. **Assyrio** is used vaguely for *Tyrio*, the famous purple. **venenum**, 'drug.' V. here uses the bad associations of the word suggestively as Ovid (*Rem. Amor.* 351) *positis sua collinet ora venenis*, of the girl who paints herself.

466. **usus olivi**, 'the oil in respect to its use'; 'the clear oil's service.' **casia** is a bark like cinnamon, which, mixed with the oil, diffuses fragrance while the lamp burns.

467. 'Repose without anxiety and a life where fraud and pretence are unknown.'

468. **dives opum variarum**, these words include food, fuel, sport, all that makes for healthy living besides beauty of surroundings. **latis otia fundis**, 'the freedom of the spacious country.' There is no allusion here to the *latifundia*, the monstrous slave-tilled estates, which were at this time destroying agriculture and imperilling the nation. V. is contrasting the confinement of city-life.

469. **vivi**, 'living,' i.e. natural lakes, opposed to the many artificial reservoirs at Rome.. V.'s birthplace was about 20 miles from the Lago di Garda. **Tempe** (plur. neut. indeclinable)

was the valley of the river Peneus between Mt Olympus and Mt Ossa in Thessaly and is a synonym in Latin poetry for any beautiful defile. **frigida Tempe**, "*frigidus*, 'cool,' constantly a word of praise in the mouth of the Italian poets: *frigidus aera vesper temperat*, G. III, 336: *frigidum Praeneste*, Hor. *Od.* III, 14: *sub urbe frigus*, Mart. IV, 64," S.

472. **exiguo**, 'to scanty fare.'

473. 'Here too is the worship of the Gods and the old are revered.'

474. 'Among them it was that Justice left her last footprints.' According to the Myth of the four Ages, gold, silver, bronze and iron, the Gods gradually left the earth which had been polluted by bloodshed and crime. The maiden Astraea, the daughter of Zeus and Themis (who personifies Law in the sense of Right, *ius* or *fas* not *lex*) remained to the last.

467–74. "Every word of these melodious and beautiful lines is telling, from the suggested contrast to Rome, with its care and hubbub (*secura quies*), its vice and fraud (*nescia fallere*), its dust and crowd (*latis otia fundis*), its artificial scenery (*vivi lacus*), its heat (*frigida Tempe*), its unsoothing sound (*mugitus boum*), its sleeplessness (*molles somni*), its sloth (*patiens operum*), its luxury (*exiguo adsueta*), and its wickedness (*sacra deum*) and loss of the old piety and dutifulness (*sanctique patres*)," S.

475–494

475–82. Here V. probably has in mind the Greek philosophic poets, Empedocles, who wrote *On Nature*, Xenophanes, also Aratus who wrote on astronomy in the 3rd century B.C.

It is evident that V. was profoundly impressed by these first attempts of Science in solving astronomic and physical problems. His admiration here and in *Ecl.* VI is sincere. At the same time he felt, and as years went on felt increasingly, that his own strength lay elsewhere. If we think of the broadening and deepening of his outlook on human life and the destiny of man, we cannot doubt that, had he been spared to devote the years after the *Aeneid* was revised to the study of philosophy as he had hoped, Plato would have become for him a stronger magnet than Epicurus.

475. **me vero**, 'as for me, first and before other things may the sweet Muses, whose priest I am, receive me graciously for the great passion that has smitten me.' The Muses are viewed as the patrons of science as well as of poetry. From youth up V. had, under Lucretius' influence, hoped to become the poet of science, but the attraction of human life and destiny was too

strong and drew him another way. **ante omnia** might be taken with *dulces*, 'Muses, sweet beyond all else to me,' but we are not warranted in taking these words intensively with an adjective.

476. **sacra fero**, lit. 'I bring offerings' =*sacerdos sum*.

477. **caeli vias et sidera**, *vias siderum in caelo*.

478. **defectus solis varios**, suggested by Lucr. v, 751 *solis item quoque defectus lunaeque latebras Pluribus e caussis fieri tibi posse putandum est*, in which *pluribus e caussis* explains *varios*. **labores**, 'agonies,' 'sufferings' of the moon when obscured in eclipse.

479. **maria alta tumescant.** These words following *tremor terris* suggest not tides but the tidal waves which follow on earthquakes as noted by Thucydides at III, 89. "Such waves were and are not infrequent in the Mediterranean, particularly near Naples where V. wrote," Haverfield.

482. **quae obstet**, 'what makes the nights move slowly.' **tardis** used proleptically in the sense of 'slow in going.' Cf. Lucr. v, 699 *propterea noctes hiberno tempore longae Cessant*.

483-4. Note the emphatic position of *frigidus*: 'But if the blood about my heart be too cold and hinder me from attaining to those depths of nature.' The heart used to be thought the seat of intelligence. Here V. has in mind the famous saying of Empedocles: "the blood about the heart is the seat of intelligence." Could we imagine Lucr. writing lines so extreme in diffidence as ll. 483-6?

486-9. This rapturous outburst is not quite consistent with grammar. Perhaps *sim* should be understood with *O* in 486, expressing a passionate wish, 'Oh to be where are the plains of Spercheos,' 'Oh for one to place me.' **Spercheos** is a river in Greece running through the fertile plain of Larissa. **bacchata**, a deponent verb used passively. **virginibus**, dative of agent in imitation of the Greek dative after a perfect passive, so at *Aen.* VI, 509 *relictum tibi*, 'omitted by thee,' and elsewhere. Cf. *Culex* 113 *gelidis bacchata iugis*, 'after revelling on the wild heights.'

488. **Taügeta**, plural of Greek *Taügeton*, later *Taügetus*, a mountain range on the west border of Laconia. **gelidis convallibus**, so l. 469 *frigida Tempe*. Mortimer Collins remarks humorously "The second *Georgic* was written in tremendously hot weather" (*Thoughts in a Garden*, vol. I, p. 63). **Haemus**, a mountain-range in Thrace, the great Balkans.

490. **qui potuit**, 'who had the gift to learn.' C. renders 'who has gained a knowledge of.'

490-2. In view of Lucr.'s dominating influence over V. it

seems idle to question whether he or some other Epicurean is
here meant. The phrases chosen by V. are what no other poet
had written or could at the time have written. Doubtless, in
the face of the anxious effort of Augustus to restore Roman
religion, it would have been impolitic to refer to Lucretius by
name. *G.* IV reminds us painfully how V. dared not oppose the
wish of the Emperor. Cf. Lucr. I, 78 *quare religio pedibus
subiecta vicissim Obteritur*; III, 37 *et metus ille foras praeceps
Acheruntis agendus Funditus humanam qui vitam turbal ab imo*;
and the Lucretian watchword (III, 1071–2); *iam rebus quisque
relictis Naturam primum studeat cognoscere rerum.* The words
rerum causas are not found in the poem. But their equivalent
is found everywhere, e.g. V, 1183–7 *praeterea caeli rationes
ordine certo Et varia annorum cernebant tempora verti Nec
poterant quibus id fieret cognoscere causis. Ergo perfugium sibi
habebant omnia divis Tradere.* The phrase reminds us of the
title of L.'s poem.

491. **fatum,** 'death.' **inexorabile,** 'relentless' probably refers
to the argument which closes Book III of Lucr.

492. **strepitum...avari.** This phrase has never been exactly
explained. **Acheron,** the mighty infernal river, must stand for
the realm of Death, always sweeping away the living. But
strepitus appeals to the imagination by calling up the loud roar
which accompanies any devouring or destructive force, for
example water or fire.

490–3. **Felix** and **fortunatus** seem practically synonymous
here, perhaps 'happy' and 'blest': even in classical Latin
beatus may convey the deeper meaning.

Munro formerly considered that these verses applied rather
to Epicurus than to Lucretius himself. But in his latest edition
he says, "I feel that by his *felix qui* V. does mean a poet-
philosopher who can only be Lucr." (See his note on I, 78.)
We may compare ll. 491–2 here with Lucr. III, 14–30 *nam
simul ac ratio tua coepit vociferari Naturam rerum, divina mente
coorta, Diffugiunt animi terrores, ... at contra nusquam
apparent Acherusia templa.*

493. **qui novit,** 'who has won the friendship of,' C.

494. **Silvanus.** Silvanus like Faunus was a spirit or deity of
the forest, belonging to the old Italian worship. Later he was
identified with Pan. "For the early settlers he was never a
peaceful inhabitant of the farm or dwelling." His domain is
the wild woodland. He is represented carrying on his shoulders
a young tree taken up by the roots. See *G.* I, 20 and *R.E.R.* pp.
76, 83–4, 132. **sorores Nymphas,** 'the sisterhood of Nymphs.'

495-542

495. **fasces populi**, 'the honours that the people confer,' i.e. the consulship of Rome, lit. 'the rods conferred by the people of Rome, who elect the consuls.' But praetors too were attended by lictors bearing the fasces, the sign of the magistrates' authority. The phrase seems suggested by Lucr. III, 996, who says that 'to beg for fasces and cruel axes from the people' means to undergo severe toil.

496-501. **flexit, doluit, invidit, carpsit**, the perfect of use or frequency which is common in the *Georgics*.

496. 'Civil feuds that provoke men to break the bonds of brotherhood.' **agitare plebem**, 'to stir up the commons' occurs in Livy III *agitatus cupiditate regni*, also found in Florus, etc. Lucr. refers pointedly to the breaking up of families owing to the civil wars, *sanguine civili rem conflant divitiasque Conduplicant avidi, caedem caede accumulantes; Crudeles gaudent in tristi funere fratris*, III, 70-3. This interpretation of the clause seems to jar with that of the passage 495-8 which deals with national dangers and anxieties rather than with strife and treachery in families. (The latter is referred to at l. 510.) Rome had suffered a great disaster in Parthia in 36 when Antony invaded the country with a splendid army, taking the side of Tiridates, who sought to wrest the throne from his brother Phraates. Antony's force met a crushing defeat and Parthia remained for long a cause of anxiety to Rome. The passage must for the meantime remain ambiguous.

497. 'Swooping down from the Danube, his sworn ally.' The Danube is in league with them because the Dacians used to cross the frozen river into Roman territory. They had long been a danger to Rome and in B.C. 30 sided with Antony in his last struggle.

498. **res R.**, 'the Roman state' in its domestic policy. **regna peritura**,'because these kingdoms must fall before Rome'; 'the doomed realms,' S.

498-9. **neque doluit miserans**, 'nor does he suffer pangs of distress over the poor.' These lines suggest an unmanly ideal of quietism and selfishness. But V.'s meaning is that the countryman, from his situation, is not brought into contact with the anxieties of empire or the misery of the poor in the great city. These do not force themselves upon him. The thought is in touch with ll. 459-60. The countryman is happy because he lives *procul discordibus armis*.

501. **tulere**, perhaps 'offer,' 'present us with.' **ipsa volentia**

sponte sua, 'cheerfully, of its own sweet will.' The accumulated
expression seems almost contradictory to passages enforcing
the toil of the farmer's life, such as *improbus labor*, I, 145. But
V. is merely emphasizing the contrast with the never-ending
strain of the ambitious man, always striving against the tide.

501. 'The iron rigours of law, the Forum with its frantic
crowds, and the Archives of the nation.' **ferrea iura**, Nettleship is inclined to render 'shameless' or 'ruthless' decisions
in the Roman courts of law (*Ancient Lives of V.* p. 57).

502. **insanum forum**, the Forum was the centre of Roman
political life, here the elections were held and its pavement was
filled with seething crowds, whose party-spirit often led to
bloodshed. **tabularia**, the Record Office was attached to the
temple of Saturn at one end of the Forum: here magistrates,
on resigning, deposited all documents connected with their
office. Mackail thinks that *vidit* (not *novit*) implies a concrete
picture and suggests as a parallel the Treasury and Record
Office with Westminster Abbey and the Houses of Parliament
all brought together in Trafalgar Square in which the general
elections, speeches and all, for the whole country are going on
(*Class. Rev.* 1896, p. 431).

503. **caeca,** 'unknown' and therefore 'dangerous.'

504. **penetrant,** 'press their way into courts and the inner
chambers of kings.' V. has probably in view Antony's intrigues
with Armenia, Egypt and other countries.

505–12. It is difficult to say whom V. has in view here.
Ambition and greed had played only too great a part in the
Roman state of his own and the previous generations. 505–6
might refer to Marius, Sulla, Catiline or Caesar according to
the side the reader takes in judging these leaders; 507 to
Lucullus or Crassus; 508 to a man like Cicero; 510 to Pompey.

505. 'Brings ruin to a city and misery to its homes.' This
might refer either to a conqueror in the civil wars entering
Rome or to the sacking of some foreign city. **peto** is thus used
with ablatives like *bello, armis, saxis.* **miseros,** used proleptically, i.e. anticipating an effect.

506. **gemma,** 'from a jewelled cup': cups were sometimes
carved out of onyx or other stones of value. Cf. *Aen.* I, 728
*hic regina gravem gemmis auroque poposcit Implevitque mero
pateram.* **Sarrano,** Sarra was an old name of Tyre.

507. **condit,** 'hoards up.' **incubat,** either literally, 'lies over his
buried gold' ("Such a mode of hoarding would be natural in
a time of proscriptions and confiscations," C.) or broods over
it as in *Aen.* VI, 610 *divitiis soli incubuere repertis Nec partem*

posuere suis, 'brood in solitude over the treasure they have gained and never share it with their kin.'

508. 'One is struck dumb with amaze at the Rostra, another, all agape, is carried away by the applause both of commons and senate as it rolls again and again along the benches.' Probably the words **stupet attonitus hiantem** are meant to convey some degree of contempt for the political aspirant who is thus obsessed by the applause given to an eloquent speaker.

509. **enim**, so at *Aen.* VIII, 84 *tibi, enim tibi,* 'to thee, even to thee,' VI, 317 *Aeneas miratus enim,* 'Aeneas marvelled indeed,' cf. the use of *enim vero,* 'of a truth.' **enim**, not here giving a reason as usual but in its old sense merely to emphasize the word. **cunei**, denotes the seats divided by gangways into wedge-shaped blocks in which the people sat while the Senators occupied the orchestra, but V. here uses *cunei* of the whole audience.

510. **gaudent perfusi**. P. is probably right in seeing here "an imitation of the Greek construction with a participle after verbs of 'feeling,' 'knowing,' etc." 'They rejoice to steep themselves.' Cf. *Aen.* II, 377 *sensit medios delapsus in hostes.*

514. 'Hence comes the toil of the year, hence the sustenance for his country and his little grandchildren, and for his herds' (for *nepotes* the Med. MS. reads *penates,* clearly a transfer from 505). The force of *patriam* is evident when we remember how Rome suffered, even as Britain has done in the World-War, through depending on foreign nations for its corn-supply. Con. says: "It is not clear whether *patriam* means his hamlet or his country. The language would point to the latter, the sense to the former." Since the year 1914 the danger of relying on corn from abroad has been brought home to us as it could not be in Conington's day. *Patria* may bear the meaning of one's native place as in Ovid, *Tristia* IV, 10, 3 *Sulmo mihi patria est.* But the tone, both in l. 514 and throughout the *Georgic,* is national rather than local: and demands the meaning 'his native land.' A man so patriotic as Virgil knew not only the material danger but realised a still greater in the degeneration which the substitution of great estates wrought by slaves for the old Italian farmers and crofters had produced in the *morale* of the nation. He saw in the return to the land the only redemption for Rome. For him one main dignity of the farmer's toil is that he supplies the food of his countrymen. Sidgwick takes *labor* as 'the produce' of the year, comparing *Aen.* VII, 248 *Iliadum labor, vestes,* 'robes, the work of Trojan dames.'

So in English we speak of a man's 'work,' meaning both the labour and the result of the labour.

515. **meritos**, 'that have served him well.'

516. **requies** is to be taken with *anno*. The phrase *nec requies*, 'there is no pause,' applies not only to the clause immediately following with *quin* which describes the fruitfulness of summer, but to the lines which follow dealing with the produce of autumn and winter. Thus C. is justified in rendering 'the stream of plenty knows no pause; the year is always teeming either with fruit or with the increase of the flock.'

519. **Sicyonia**, because Sicyon, a small state in the north-east of Peloponnesus, was famous for its olives.

520. **laeti**, 'sleek from their acorn-feast': used, of flocks at l. 144, in the same way as V. often applies it to rich and fertile fields. **dant arbuta silvae**, 'there are arbutes in the woods for the picking.' The sensitiveness of C. to the value of one word rather than another in a phrase like this is worth noting by the young student: **dant** means something more than 'yield': rather 'make a present of.'

521. **ponit**, 'drops at his feet.' Cf. *fundit* at 460.

522. **mitis...coquitur**, 'is being baked into ripeness.' **saxis** referring to the vineyards on rock-terraces, cf. l. 377.

523. With **interea** V. passes from the fruitfulness without to the farmer's happiness within his home: **circum oscula**, 'about his lips' for kisses, cf. Gray's *Elegy*, "and climb his knees the envied kiss to share."

524. **domus** may mean either 'home' or 'wife,' cf. *domus te nostra tota salutat* Cic., *tota domus duo sunt* Ovid, but it is less forced to take *domus* here as a personification, 'His chaste home preserves its purity as of old.' **servat**, 'keeps the tradition of,' C.

527. **ipse**, 'the master.'

528. **coronant**, 'wreathe the bowl with flowers' as was the custom at feasts, cf. *Aen.* III, 525 *magnum cratera corona Induit implevitque mero*. **ubi ignis in medio** must be taken with the words preceding 'stretched along the grass where a fire burns in the midst.' **ignis**, the fire is burning on an altar of turf.

530. **ponit certamina iaculi**. Here we have one of those condensed phrases which form a chief difficulty in V.'s style. *Ponere certamina* is the technical phrase for 'to appoint a contest,' cf. *Aen.* v, 66 *prima Teucris ponam certamina classis*, but *ponere* has to do a double duty in the sense 'to set up a mark on the elm to be aimed at.' The phrase *ponere certamina*

is probably borrowed from the Greek ἀγῶνα προτιθέναι: *instituere* is more common in this sense. Such double meaning can rarely be conveyed in rendering.

531. **praedura**, 'hard as iron.'

532-3. **hanc vitam**, 'such was the life.' **sic scilicet**, 'thus assuredly.' *Scilicet* explains or adds a detail to a previous statement, as here to the praise of old Italy.

535. **una**, 'yet remained a single city.' This line is repeated in Anchises' prophecy of 'our glorious Rome' at *Aen.* VI, 783. Virgil justly lays stress on this union of the seven hill-fortresses. As Freeman says, this is "the first instance of that inherent power of assimilation or incorporation on the part of the Roman commonwealth, which went on alike under Kings, Consuls and Caesars." *Histor. Essays*, II, p. 252.

536-8. **etiam**, connecting with what precedes, 'nay.' **Dictaei regis**, Jupiter who was said to have been born at Mt Dicte in Crete and succeeded Saturn as king in Latium. **impia**, because of old the ox, as man's fellow-labourer, was regarded as sacred and, as Cicero tells us, it was thought impiety to eat its flesh (*De Nat. D.* II, 63). **aureus**, 'the monarch of the Golden Age,' C.

Dr Warde Fowler writes: "Saturn was the deity, I think, both of the operation of sowing and of the sown seed, now (at the time of the Saturnalia held in December) reposing in the bosom of mother earth." Varro says, "Ab satu dictus Saturnus." He was in later times identified with Kronos, the father of Zeus, but, as Fowler says, "there is no real proof of this." Regarding such adjectival names as Saturnus, Neptunus, Portunus, Volcanus, etc. he adds, "These are not proper names, but clearly express some character or function exercised by the power or *numen* to whom the name is given." [Dr Fowler defines *numen* as 'a being with a will': *nuere* means 'to exercise will-power.'] Saturnus is the most familiar example; the word suggests no personality, but rather a sphere of operations (whether we take the name as referring to sowing or to seed maturing in the soil) in which a certain *numen* is helpful See *R.E.R.* pp. 100, 111, 118. See also *Religion of Ancient Rome*, by Cyril Bailey, 1911: "The characteristic appellation of a divine spirit in the oldest stratum of the Roman religion is not *deus*, a god, but rather *numen*, a power: he becomes *deus* when he obtains a name and so is on the way to obtaining a definite personality."..."For 170 years, Varro tells us,...the Romans worshipped the gods without images....The genuine Roman theology has no gods of human form with human relations to one another...but only these impersonal individualities, if we may so call them, capable of no relation to one another but able to bring good or ill to men," pp. 12–17.

539, **audierant.** Note the semi-impersonal use of the third plural answering to the French 'on.' It is not uncommon in the *Aen.* as at 1, 638. **etiam,** again as at 536, connects with what precedes. C. renders 'In days before the rule of the Cretan king ...days when the blast of the trumpet, etc....were sounds unknown.'

541. 'But we have now traversed a distance boundless in its circuits.' **aequor** denotes any level surface whether land or sea: cf. *G.* ii, 105 *Libyci aequoris*, of the Libyan desert. **spatia** is used by V. sometimes for the circuits in the race-course, sometimes for the passage of the racers round them. Seven laps had to be traversed by the chariots in the circus at Rome. *G.* 1 also concludes with the metaphor of a chariot-race but in a quite different application.

GEORGIC III

The third book deals with breeding cattle, V. mentions the principal deities presiding over this. He complains that the old legends, so often treated by the poets of the day, had been worn threadbare. "These could once have captivated idle minds with the spell of poetry but now they are all hackneyed," *omnia iam vulgata*. The touch about idle minds recalls to us Morris's phrase, too unjust to himself, "The idle singer of an empty day." But the fault was not with the beautiful Greek myths, out of which Aeschylus and Sophocles had built noble dramas, but with the Roman poetaster, who had exploited them after the unreal fashion of the time. Life had become too serious a matter for V. since the days when he had been the singer of Amaryllis. He must now try a new path to fame dealing with the glories of Rome and Augustus' great conquests. Here again is a sign of the poet's growth in mind and soul. He must reflect the life and problems of his own day. See note on II, 45–6.

1–16, 26–33 ff.

1–2. **Pales** was the rural deity of shepherds and flocks whose festival was on the 21st April. By the river **Amphrysus** in Thessaly Apollo fed the flocks of King Admetus, in order to atone for his killing the Cyclops. **Lycaeus**, the mountain in Arcadia, was the original seat of Pan's worship.

4. **Eurystheus**, King of Mycenae, was the task-master who ordained the labours of Hercules.

5. **Busiris**, the cruel King of Egypt, who sacrificed all strangers till Hercules came, who was seized like the rest but broke his bonds and slew the king. illaudati, 'detested,' a strong affirmative expressed by negation of the contrary.

6. **Hylas**, a beautiful boy who sailed in the Argo. He went to fetch water, but the nymphs loved him and drew him down. On **Delos** Latona gave birth to Apollo and Artemis. So far as we know no Latin poet deals with these myths. Thus it must be Greek poets that V. has in view. cui, dative of agent after participle, a construction borrowed from the Greek.

7. humero eburno. Tantalus killed his son Pelops and served up his flesh at a banquet to the Gods, who restored him to life and replaced with ivory the portion eaten.

9, 10. The last words are adopted from Ennius' epitaph, *volito vivu' per ora virum,* 'from lip to lip.' Usually *per ora* means 'before' or 'past the faces of men.' Thus the phrase would mean 'soar in the air in the sight of men.' But elsewhere it is used in the sense to pass from mouth to mouth in talk. C. says this seems to be one of the passages where V. "shadows out more meanings than one without discriminating them sharply in his own mind." See his note here and on *Aen.* II, 11. The metaphor, bringing the Muses captive from Helicon, is borrowed from a Roman triumph. **Aonio,** from Aonia, a part of Boeotia, where were Mt Helicon and the spring, Aganippe, the haunt of the Muses.

In what follows, 16–33, V. promises to write a poem in honour of Augustus. The poet is to return from Greece in triumph, bringing palms of victory, to found by his native stream a temple to Augustus, bearing the Emperor's exploits carved on its doors. Under the allegory of a temple he refers to the *Aeneid.* **primus** (l. 10) does not refer to rural poetry but to an epic not yet begun, *modo vita supersit.* The temple is to be adorned with sculptures commemorating the world-wide victories won under Julius Caesar and Augustus, from Britain to the Nile and Parthia; the last of these, won by Tiberius, did not occur till about 20 B.C., and V.'s reference to it must have been added shortly before his death.

12. **Idumaea,** the Edom of Scripture, south-west of Judaea, was famous for its palm-trees.

16. **Caesar.** The name 'Augustus' does not occur in the *Georgics.* The emperor did not assume it until more than three years after the battle of Actium, in January 27 B.C. (*Aeneas at the Site of Rome,* p. 111). **in medio,** the central shrine of the temple is to contain his statue.

26. **auro, elephanto.** V. here recalls the two most majestic masterpieces of Greek sculpture; Phidias's statues of Athena in the Parthenon and Zeus at Olympia. Both were wrought in gold and ivory, in the use of which Phidias excelled.

27. **Gangaridum,** contr. from *Gangaridarum,* an Indian people living near the Ganges' mouth: they represent the defeat of Antony's Eastern allies.

28. **undantem bello,** 'swelling high with war,' i.e. with warlike feeling in the rising under Cleopatra.

29. **navali aere,** 'of the brass of captured vessels.'

30. **Niphaten,** a mountain of Armenia.

31. **Parthum,** as Augustus did not conquer the Parthians nor were the lost standards recovered by Tiberius till 20 B.C.,

we must suppose that these lines, if not an intentional exaggeration, were added after the completion of the poem.

33. **utroque ab litore**, 'on two opposite coasts' from Spain to Syria. "In these lines the poet depicts the subjection by Augustus of divers nations and countries, viz. (1) India, (2) Egypt, (3) Asia, (4) Armenia, (5) Parthia, and (6) more generally and vaguely, the East and West (*utroque ab litore... diverso ex hoste*) i.e. Europe and Asia," S.

46–8. **accingar dicere**. Infinitive of purpose, a poetical usage. The infinitive is used by V. after many verbs which usually take *ut*, e.g. *Aen.* I, 527 *Libycos populare Penates, venimus*. See Madvig, § 389.

47. **nomen ferre**, 'to waft his name down centuries long as those which separate the cradle of Tithonus from Caesar himself,' C. Dr Fowler is disposed to think that the picture of Augustus on the Shield in *Aen.* VIII, "enthroned in an unfinished temple, accepting the free-will offerings of peoples, coming from the far limits of the Empire...is a fragment of the poem, projected in *Geor.* III, 46, and may in its original form have been written between 31 and 29 B.C.," i.e. before the triple triumph of Augustus. The tone of joy and exultation in V.'s pictures both in the *Georgic* and on the Shield would suggest that they belong to 29 B.C., that year of happiness and rejoicing (*Aeneas at the Site of Rome*, pp. 121–2).

Sidgwick holds that, if written in 29 B.C., the poetic exaggeration would be excessive, since Augustus had had no fight with Indians at all, never subdued Asia, or beaten back Niphates or the Parthian. He therefore attributes them to 31 as a forecast of future triumphs due to the exultation of the time. Page holds the lines to refer to Augustus' visit to the East in 21 and his sending a victorious expedition to Parthia under Tiberius in 20, so that this passage is due to a later revision and was added by Virgil shortly before his death in 19 B.C.

72–94

72. **pecus equinum** here means 'the stud,' horses for breeding.

73. **submitto**, technical term, 'to rear' for the hope of a new race.

75. **continuo**, 'from the first,' its meaning is defined here by the preceding words *a teneris* not, as often in V., by what follows. See note on I, 356. **pecoris g. pullus**, 'a colt of a well-bred family.'

76. **mollia**, 'in an elastic way.' **reponit** seems to answer to *altius ingreditur* in the sense of 'sets down.' The phrase *mollia*

crura reponit is used by Ennius of cranes. P. says: "There is nothing more noticeable about a young thoroughbred than the clean way in which it picks up its feet and the lightness with which it puts them down."

78. **audet**, 'has the courage.'

79. **nec horret**, 'does not start at.'

80. **argutum**, 'clean-cut,' 'fine-shaped.' See note on 1, 143. "Varro and Columella recommend a small head," C. Horace, *Sat.* 1, 2, 89, mentions *breve caput* as a good point.

82. "*spadices* are bay, Xenophon's favourite colour, *glauci* are either bay or blue-roan," Royds.

84. **mico**, used of swift movement, 'to twitch.'

85. **collectum ignem**, 'and gathered fire.' Royds says: "The red dilated nostril of the excited or 'blowing' horse is a sufficient explanation." "His nostrils drink the air and forth again, As from a furnace, vapours doth he send" (*Venus and Adonis*). The picture of the war-horse in Job xxxix, 19–25 is worth comparing. **fremens**, a correction in the Medicean, is more natural, but *premens*, 'compressing,' is found in all the MSS.

87. **duplex spina**, "a backbone sunk between two ridges of flesh," Royds. Such a hollow spine is opposed to *extans* in Varro II, 7, 5.

88. **solido...cornu**, 'has the deep ring of solid horn,' C., who adds: "A hard and thick hoof would be especially requisite when horses are not shod with iron."

89. **domitus habenis**, 'tamed to the rein.' Castor and Pollux were demi-gods, sons of Zeus, born of Leda at Amyclae in Laconia, and therefore brothers of Helen. Their steeds, Xanthus and Cyllarus, were presented to them by Neptune. They were specially patrons of the Equites at Rome, who for three centuries honoured them by a solemn procession through the city and past their temple. Castor was the more famous as a horseman, Pollux as a boxer.

91. **currus**, 'the pair'; they were named Xanthus and Balius. Cf. 1, 514, for *currus*, 'the team.'

93–4. Saturn was said to be in love with the nymph, Philyra (mother of the famous Centaur, Chiron), and, when surprised by his wife, Rhea, to have escaped in the form of a horse.

284–293

284. **irreparabile**, 'not to be recalled.'

285. **capti amore**, 'beguiled by love of my subject.' **circumvectamur** generally taken as a metaphor either from sailing

(e.g. *c. Ligurem oram*, Livy XLI, 17) or riding. *Circumvector* has the meaning 'to travel about,' 'visit in succession,' e.g. with *oppida*, Plautus, *Rud.* IV, 2. Servius explains it, "Dum speciatim cuncta describimus."

286. **superat** for *superest*. **curae**, 'of my task.'

287. **agitare**, 'to treat of,' lit. 'to occupy oneself with.' V. not infrequently uses a word capable of more than one application: *agitare* might here apply either to the farmer or to the poet.

288. V. could not have considered the care of sheep and goats more laborious or more honourable than that of horses and kine. "We must therefore consider this line as a mere transition to what follows, viz. the difficulty which the poet finds in conferring dignity on so humble a subject," K.

289. **magnum quam sit**, 'how hard a task it is to overcome the difficulties of subject and to invest a theme so slender with the dignity of poetry.' At the opening of the fourth *Georgic*, V. refers in a memorable line to the *Admiranda tibi levium spectacula rerum*, difficulty of handling small themes so that they shall be worthy of verse. Here we have the old locative case as preserved in certain phrases not referring specially to place: e.g. *victus animi, nec me animi fallit, animi pendere*, and also used along with a great number of adjectives; *dubius animi* therefore means 'in mind' not 'in respect of mind.' See S.

291. Here again we have echoes of Lucretius: *avia Pieridum peragro loca nullius ante Trita solo. iuvat integros accedere fontis ...Insignemque meo capiti petere inde coronam, Unde prius nulli velarint tempora Musae*, Lucr. I, 926. See Introduction, § III.

292. **iuga**, 'the heights,' are contrasted with *mollis clivus*.

293. **Castaliam**, a fountain in Parnassus, sacred to Apollo and the Muses; Lucretius just cited prefers to speak of 'new fountains,' not like V. of finding a new road to the old Castalian spring. **devertitur**, 'turns aside.' V. is resolved not to follow the beaten track 'of former poets.' He will take a bypath of his own.

515–530

515. **ecce autem**, introducing a new object 'look there.' **duro**, 'stubborn'; the ox struggles to pull under the weight of the plough.

517. **it tristis**, 'moves sadly away,' C., 'advancing unyokes,' Mackail.

518. **abiungens**, the present participle is used in a lax way

for the past, Latin having no aorist participle. Cf. *G.* IV, 513
and a glaring instance at *Aen.* III, 305. Page notes the extraordinary condensation with which V. suggests three complete
pictures in 517-19, the disheartened ploughman, the bereaved
steer and the furrow left half-finished.

518. **fraterna morte.** Note the epithet. George Sand has
brought out its force in the well-known opening of *La Mare au
Diable*. Two such oxen, she says, are called in France 'brothers.'
When one dies, the other refuses to work with a new companion
and allows itself to die of grief. He remains in the stable, thin
and wasted, beating his flanks with his tail, breathing with
distaste upon the fodder set before him, with eyes always
turning towards the door, scraping with his hoof the empty
stall at his side and calling for his lost yoke-fellow with pitiful
lowings. "The cowherd will say 'It is a pair of oxen lost. His
brother is dead and this one will work no more:...he will not
eat and soon he will be dead of hunger.'"

520-3. The suggestion of these lines is in Lucr. II, 361-3,
the cow robbed of her calf and searching for it everywhere:
*nec tenerae salices atque herbae rore vigentes Fluminaque illa
queunt summis labentia ripis Oblectare animum subitamque
avertere curam.* 'Nor can the soft willows and grass quickened
with dew and yon rivers gliding level with their banks comfort
her mind and put away the care that has entered into her.'

520-30. These beautiful lines refer of course to the ox which
has fallen dying, but they go back rather abruptly to earlier
scenes and stages of the disease in the river-side meadow.
Both Lucretius and Virgil are full of sympathy for the distress
of the animal creation. The touch of pity for the undeserved
suffering of the benefactor of man is truly Virgilian but the
older poet is, as usual, the more vivid of the two.

522. C. remarks that, in deviating from Lucr. above quoted,
"Virgil has perhaps thought rather of what would charm a
spectator than of what would attract cattle....The words *qui—
amnis* show a genuine feeling for the picturesque."

purior electro, 'more transparent than amber.' The chief
features of a mountain stream, tumbling down among its
boulders, are its perfect clearness and its amber tinge. Haverfield prefers to take *electrum* as meaning the metal, an alloy
of gold and silver. But the polished surface of a metal can only
reflect the light, whereas water becomes radiant through and
through. The imagination rejects such a simile.

523. **solvuntur**, 'are relaxed,' 'hang slack.' **ima**, 'at the
extremity' of the flank, implying 'from end to end.'

524. **fluit** means 'gradually sinking' as in the case of the dying Camilla. *Ad terram non sponte fluens, Aen.* XI, 828.

527. **repostae** may mean either 'renewed,' i.e. 'a succession of' or 'replenished,' i.e. banquets of many courses; *simplicis* in 528 would support the latter.

529. **exercita cursu**, 'rapid running (and therefore 'fresh') rivers': *exercita*, 'driven' is used by Lucretius of swift and constant motion as of the atoms, *adsiduo varioque exercita motu* at II, 97.

530. **abrumpit**, 'breaks short.'

GEORGIC IV

1–7

1–2. **protinus**, 'next in order I shall advance to that gift of Heaven, honey dropping from the sky.' **exsequi**, in the sense of going right through a subject. **coelestia**, partly in the sense of *aerii*, partly as being the gift of the Gods. Honey was believed to fall like dew on the leaves whence the bees gathered it. Thus even Aristotle speaks of 'honey which falls from the air' (*Hist. An.* v, 22). **mellis**, explanatory genitive.

3. Excellently rendered by the writer of *Lorna Doone*, "The admirable drama of small things." We may compare III, 290 when V. avows his effort *angustis hunc addere rebus honorem*. **levium**, of course in the sense 'things slight in themselves.' V. is very conscious of the difficulty of treating the subject in a poem.

4. 'the high-souled leaders.' The playful tone noted at I, 119 is very noticeable when V. treats of the bees, exaggerating the parallel with human ways, as at 29 where Neptuno, "the Ocean," denotes a tiny rill near the hive, a battle between two swarms described with full military detail at 67–87, the unresting workers building the comb compared to the toiling Cyclopes at 176, and so on. **ordine**, 'successively.'

5. **mores**, 'character.' **studia**, 'tastes and habits.' **populos**, 'the races.'

6. **si quem**, characteristic of V.'s tact; he will not speak of fame for himself, but for any one who may succeed, 'if there be any one whom adverse deities allow (to undertake the task).'

7. **laeva**, Servius followed by some scholars renders 'propitious,' but V. uses the word in the favourable sense only of thunder on the left, while **sinunt** is more naturally used of adverse Gods.

8–50

9. **sit**, subj. of purpose.

11–12. Before *insultent* and *decutiat, ubi* must be understood from *quo*.

13–14. **picti terga, signata pectus**, accusatives after a passive verb, a construction borrowed from Greek. Cf. *Ecl.* III, 106 *inscripti nomina regum, Aen.* II, 273 *per pedes traiectus lora.* **squalentia**, 'rough,' would appear to be used here = *squamosa*, 'scaly.'

15. **Procne**, the Athenian wife of the Thracian prince Tereus. In order to avenge his violence towards her sister,

Philomela, she slew her son and gave his flesh as food to Tereus. At *Ecl.* VI, 78 V. seems to invert the names of wife and sister, 'what kind of banquet and present Philomela got ready for Tereus.' When pursued by her husband Procne was turned into a swallow and Philomela into a nightingale. The myth of course reflects the belief that the nightingale's song expresses sadness, a notion which Coleridge in his fine poem *The Nightingale* distinctly rejects, and calls a mere 'conceit.' "It is of course the male bird that sings and his song is not inspired by sorrow" (Royds, p. 54). In point of fact the common swallow has a deep red patch upon its throat which the myth explains as the sign of a bloody deed. **aliae volucres et Procne.** K. renders *et* 'especially.' Royds protests, "The swallow tribe do little harm, only catching bees occasionally," p. 59.

16. **omnia vastant,** 'they spread havoc'; a general term, simply denoting what is more precisely phrased in the following *ipsas—escam.* **volantes** is commonly taken as a substantive here like *balantum,* 'sheep' (after Lucretius), in *G.* I, 272 or *volitans,* 'an insect,' in III, 147, but it simply means here 'on the wing.'

19. **tenuis,** 'shallow.' **fugiens,** 'stealing.'

21. **reges,** the queen-bee was regarded as the male by the ancients, except as some fancy by Xenophon (*Oec.* VII, 17).

22. **vere suo,** 'the time when they are in vigour after their winter seclusion,' C., who renders 'in the spring they love.' So P. and Pap. *suus* is not, I think, used here in the sense of *sopor suus* at l. 190, where see note. K. explains the phrase 'when they feel the weather warm enough to work in.'

23. **decedere calori,** 'to take refuge from the heat,' cf. *Ecl.* VIII, 88 *decedere nocti,* 'to retire before the night.'

24. **obvia.** Note the position of the word. 'And a tree may be in the way to detain them under its leafy shelter.'

26. **grandia saxa,** 'mighty rocks.'

29. **Neptuno,** 'the Ocean.' The playful grandiloquence seems intended *angustis addere rebus honorem* (III, 290). Varro speaks of throwing in *lapillos* and says that the rivulet must not be more than two or three inches deep (III, 16).

30. **casiae virides,** referred to in *G.* II, 213 as *casiae humiles,* where it is coupled with *ros* which Servius identifies with *ros marinum,* 'rosemary.'

31. **serpyllum,** 'wild thyme.' **thymbrae,** 'savory'; note that all three plants are strong-scented.

32. **irriguum** has an active force, 'the spring that waters the spot.' So *rigui amnes,* 'the rivers that freshen the valleys.'

33. **corticibus suta cavatis.** In the north of Scotland bee-hives are said to be made from the rough fibres of the fir-wood found in peat-mosses.

34. **alvaria,** not *alvearia,* is probably correct: *alvus,* 'the belly' fem. and *alveus,* 'a hollow vessel' are often confused. *alvus* is the regular word for a 'hive.' *alvare* would mean the whole apiary, more hives than one.

36. **remittit,** the opposite of *cogit; liquefacta remittit,* 'thaws it and makes it run.'

38. **nequiquam** does not mean 'without an object' but 'without result' as l. 45 shows. "The bees take good care of themselves, but you should care for them nevertheless," C. Hence V. uses *tamen* at l. 45. **tenuia.** Dactyl scanned as *tenwia; u* and *i* are spirants and may have the force either of vowels or consonants as here. See note on 1, 482.

39. **fuco et floribus,** hendiadys. The word *fucus* means (1) a lichen, (2) the dye extracted from this or other plants: rouge for the complexion, (3) disguise or pretence of any kind. C. renders 'with the pollen of flowers' which may be V.'s meaning. Bee-keeping was in part the calling of V.'s father. In reality bees use for this purpose not the pollen or coloured dust from the stamens of flowers but what is called propolis, a reddish-brown resin gathered chiefly from the buds of poplars, chestnut trees and pines, but also from the gum exuding from the trunks. This substance is extremely glutinous, *visco lentius.* **oras,** 'the entrance of the hive,' K. C. says: "*Explent* would point rather to crevices, *spiramenta,* though no instance is given of *orae* in this sense."

42. **effossis latebris.** "This is an error if it means that the honey-bee excavates for himself. His natural home is a hollow tree" (Royds, *Beasts, Birds and Bees of Virgil,* 1918).

43. **fovere,** gnomic perfect, 'they keep their home warm': this is the root idea of the word: thus we have *sol fovet, pennis fovent* of hens with chickens, then 'to cherish,' 'fondle,' as in *gremio fovet* of the boy Ascanius in the lap of Dido. **larem,** 'home,' here as at *G.* III, 344. This metaphorical use of Lar is not to be found in the *Aeneid* where, as Dr Fowler says, "it is a word of serious religious and historical import." The Lar was originally a Deity not of the house but of the land belonging to it: he was the only Deity of the farm whom the slaves were permitted to worship, hence called *Lar familiaris,* and through them found his way into the house as the cha-racteristic deity of Roman private worship, *R.E.R.* pp. 77–9.

48. **cancros...paludi.** The objection is to the strong odour.

Acc. to Pliny the smoke ascending from burnt crabs was thought a remedy for some diseases of trees and the ashes good for certain human ailments, H. Pliny tells us that bees attack persons who use strong perfumes and Columella that they are angry with those who smell of wine.

49. **coeni**, mire or filth of any kind. **sonant pulsu**, 'ring with the impact of sound.' "The question whether bees hear is still unsettled," Royds, p. 64.

50. Lit. 'and the echo of the voice striking (the rock) rebounds.' **offendor** is here used in a middle sense, 'to strike against.' But it is not the echo which strikes the rock but the sound itself, *vox*. This is an instance of transference of subject. Another notable instance occurs at *Aen.* v, 150, of the cheering at the naval race, *pulsati colles clamore resultant*, literally, 'the hill-sides buffeted by the shouting rebound.' The hills do not rebound but it is the shouting which rebounds from them. The object acted on changes places with the actor. The expression adds vividness. Cf. the phrase, 'The walls dance in the flickering fire-light.' The transference of the epithet is also common in V. Thus at *Aen.* vi, 374, *amnem severum Eumenidum*, where *severus* properly applies to the Furies, at 453 *obscuram* agrees with Dido when it strictly refers to the dim place where she is seen, at 543 *impia Tartara* where the adjective belongs not to the place but to its inhabitants. These two forms of indirect expression contribute largely to make V. so difficult to translate.

51–66

51. **quod superest**, 'moreover' or 'to continue': a somewhat prosaic phrase of which Lucr. is fond.

52. 'Has thrown wide open the gate of heaven with its summer light,' **luce**, not, I think, 'by force of summer's rays' as C.: *luce* expresses accompaniment rather than cause here.

53. **saltus**, 'lawns' or 'glades.'

54. **metunt**, 'reap their harvest from,' **purpureos**, here 'bright': as a colour term, its meaning is very wide, as Horace's *purpureus olor* (of the swan) reminds us. "*Flumina libant* is not true," says Royds, "for bees do not drink on the wing."

55–8. **hinc**, thrice, 'hence it is that' or 'therefore.' Their activity in the hive, rearing the young, building their combs and sending out swarms is the outcome of the warm weather and of their banquet on the flowers.

57. **excudunt**, lit. 'hammer out,' hence used of metal work at *Aen.* vii, 848, and used also of 'hatching' chickens from the egg and of 'composing' a writing.

61. **contemplator**, 'mark them well.' Notice the arresting effect of this word and the pause. This lengthened form of imperative is used formally in laws. Lucretius uses it with great effect to call attention to some illustration of special value for his argument, so at II, 114 of the motes seen in the sunbeam in connection with his Atomic Theory, or at VI, 189 of the piled-up clouds as bearing on his explanation of thunder. Here V.'s point is that if you watch you will see that the bees 'always make for fresh water and the shelter of trees.'

62. **huc**, on the place which they make for. **sapor** commonly = 'taste' 'savour' but also as here 'scent.'

63. **melisphyllum**, contr. for *melissophyllum*, Gk., 'bees-leaf,' 'balm.' **cerinthae**, 'honey-wort,' acc. to Sargeaunt. It is named from the white wax-like spots on the leaves (from *cera*, Greek κηρός, bees-wax). **ignobile**, probably 'common.'

Note the reference at l. 64 to the worship of the Magna Mater, Cybele, one of the Oriental religions which were rapidly spreading through Italy. V. speaks here of the *cymbala Matris* as if these rites were familiar to all. These two words are V.'s only reference to the new worship which impressed Lucretius so profoundly by its imposing processions with wild intoxicating music and frenzied dances and also by the awe-struck crowds who looked on. We should have liked to know how one so sympathetic with all human feelings and needs as V. was impressed by the sight. It is significant of the new religious cravings in their better aspects that the worship of the Mother of the Gods was solemnly inaugurated at Rome in 230 B.C. by so noble a man as Scipio the elder, whom Fowler calls "that strange soldier mystic, the great Scipio" (*R.E.R.* p. 330).

65. Note the force of *ipsae*, repeated 'unbidden they will settle,' C., 'without any further labour on your part,' as K. explains.

66. **condent se**, 'they will nestle.'

67–87

67. Note the emphatic position of **ad pugnam**, 'But if 'tis for battle that they have gone forth from the hive.' The sentence is an 'anacolouthon,' lacking a principal clause. The parenthesis introduced by *nam saepe*, 'for as often happens,' expands into a paragraph. **duobus regibus**, 'when there are two kings.'

69–70. 'And at once you may forecast even from far away (i.e. by the sound) the temper of the mass and that their hearts are throbbing for war.' So C. who compares *Aen.* VII, 482 *belloque animos accendit agrestes*, explaining the term *in bellum*.

71. **Martius canor**, a comparison as the next line shows.

72. **fractos sonitus** 'the short repeated blasts.'

73. **trepidae** combines two notions, 'in eager alarm they flock together.' The word **corusco** expressing rapid motion naturally acquires the meaning 'to flash' since rapid motion in the light causes a gleam. See l. 98.

74. The first clause can only mean 'sharpen their stings with their beaks.' The sting of a bee is in its tail, so that V.'s mistake is a gross one. Royds says that probably he "misunderstood the cleaning of the antennae with their legs which is part of every bee's toilette." **aptantque lacertos**, 'brace up their arms for the fight.'

77. **sudum**, 'rainless,' 'fine.' **campos patentes**, 'an open field' simply because bees do not venture out in rain; stragglers are rarely caught in a shower. *campus* is used to mean 'the battle-field' as frequently in Corn. Nepos. The two words seem to have passed into a phrase like our own 'a free field,' as at *Aen.* v, 553, when Aeneas orders the ground to be cleared for the youths' evolutions on horseback, *campos iubet esse patentes*. C. explains *patentes* as apparently meaning 'the air cleared from storms.' But the words seem here used rather as a common phrase.

78. **concurritur.** Other instances of intransitive verbs used impersonally in the passive occur at l. 189 of this *Georgic*, *siletur*, 374 *perventum est*.

79. **mixtae**, 'crowding together.'

80–1. These lines are a poetical fiction for bees do not fight 'on the wing,' Royds. The actual fighting by stings takes place on the ground. **tantum glandis**, 'such a shower of acorns,' *glandis* being used collectively. "Servius reminds us that in the encounters of bees slayers perish as well as slain," C.

82. **ipsi**, the two kings, "the *reges* upon whom the whole paragraph turns," C.

83. "**versant** may be no more than a poetical equivalent for *habent*, but it may also refer to the plans which the generals are supposed to form with their minds active in the excitement of the combat," C., who compares *Aen.* IV, 630 *partes animum versabat in omnes* which he renders 'she whirled her thought to this side and to that' (of Dido's excited thought before she resolves to take her own life).

84. **usque adeo** may be used without a following clause explaining the degree, as at *Ecl.* I, 12. Kennedy explains it as

"a demonstrative antecedent to *dum*," and views *subegit* as a syncopated form of *subegerit*. But this is unnecessary for the verb here expresses not a purpose but a result, 'Resolute to flinch not to the last till a crushing victory has driven,' etc. Pap. **obnixus** has here no participial force such as 'striving' but simply as an adjective 'firm-set,' 'steadfast.' So at Livy VI, 12 *obnixos vos stabili gradu hostium impetum excipere.*

86–7. "These outbursts of the soul, this awful riot—Toss up a pinch of dust and all is quiet." Blackmore.

87. **pulveris iactu.** Is it necessary to see here any intention to recall a parallel in the last solemn rite of Roman burial, *iniecto ter pulvere*? I think not. The two words might suggest it, but the note is out of keeping with the tone of the passage which is humour, with a touch of pathos, but not seriousness. Virgil is too much of a poet to moralize in the act of giving a useful hint to the bee-keeper.

116–148

116–148. Conington calls this passage "a graceful inter-position, sketching the plan for what might have been a fifth *Georgic*." Most scholars follow Servius in regarding this man as probably one of the Cilician pirates whom Pompey, after conquering them, settled in Calabria. Corycus was a city on the sea-shore of Cilicia. The Cilicians were famous for their skill in gardening and used to grow plants in greenhouses, roofed with plates of mica instead of glass.

116. **equidem,** though V. often uses it with the 1st person, has no connection with *ego*. V. has just recommended the bee-keeper to cultivate flowers and continues, 'I should myself have liked to write on the subject of gardening.'

118. **colendi,** seems almost pleonastic. **rosaria** may depend either on *ornaret* or on *canerem*; *ni traham...canerem.* "The proper tense in both clauses would be the imperfect sub-junctive, to denote a present condition which is no longer possible ('Were I not furling sail, I should be singing'): for the sake of vividness and variety, the present tense is substituted in the protasis ('should I not furl') as though the alternative were still possible," Pap.

120. **potis rivis,** 'in drinking of the stream.'

121. **apium (gauderet) ripis** would be more usual but less characteristic of V. Cf. *G.* II, 112 *litora myrtetis laetissima.* This use is an outcome of his strong sense of Life, mysteriously present in the whole of Nature, e.g. in the love of plants for certain habitats, as *amantes litora myrtos*, l. 124.

122. **in ventrem.** Evidently this applies not to a cucumber but to a gourd or marrow. **sera comantem,** the neuter plural of the adjective is here used as an adverb, like *grave olentia* at l. 270, *suave rubens* at *Ecl.* III, 63. **comantem,** 'flowering.' Cf. l. 137 *comam.*

123. **acanthi.** See n. on II, 119.

125. **Oebaliae,** i.e. Tarentum, founded by a Laconian colony. Oebalus was a mythical king of Sparta.

126. **niger Galaesus.** As Italian rivers are so often turbid, *niger* might almost answer to our own 'clear' in opposition to the *flavus Tibris.* The Galaesus in Calabria still bears the same character. Note the contrast between 'dark' stream and the golden harvest-fields. Blackmore renders 'where black Galaesus lips the harvest-gold.'

127. **relicti,** 'waste' or 'unappropriated.' The land was unoccupied, as Keightley suggests, "either as is most probable on account of its worthlessness or as being *subsicivus,* i.e. a patch left out by the surveyors when measuring out land to the *coloni.*"

128. **fertilis,** either 'productive under grazing' or taking *iuvencis = arando,* 'fruitful for ploughing.' The second meaning, followed by C. and Pap., makes V.'s statement more comprehensive of the general uses of land; **pecori** would then include grazing for cattle or for sheep. Salmasius for this reason conjectured *Cereri* for *pecori.* **illa** is here emphatic, 'land like that.'

129. **seges** means both 'sown land' as here, and the 'crop' itself.

130. **rarum,** 'here and there.' **circum,** 'round the beds of vegetables.' **in dumis,** in connection with the two preceding lines, seems to mean that the soil was only fit to grow thorns which still shot up in it.

131. **verbenas,** usually in plural, is applied to foliage of various kinds used in sacred rites; especially the olive, bay or myrtle. But it was also used to denote a single plant, which has not been identified. **vescus,** commonly explained 'fineseeded.' The exact meaning was a puzzle to the ancient grammarians: it seems to range between 'fine' as poppy-seed and 'slender' or 'slight' as of the willow leaf at *G.* III, 175. On the Continent poppy-seeds are often sprinkled thickly on the top of rolls before they are baked, which gives an agreeable flavour. At Lucr. I, 326 *vesco sale saxa peresa,* Munro renders the phrase 'fine, small spray.'

132. **animis,** 'he matched in his pride the wealth of kings.'

136. **cursus,** 'the rush.'

137. **tondebat**, short, final syllable again lengthened in *arsi*: similarly *fultus hyacintho* at *Ecl.* VI, 43 before the four-syllable Greek word.

138. **increpitans.** Note the force of the frequentative, 'chiding many a time the summer for its lateness and the west winds for lagging behind.'

139. **fetis** either 'breeding' or 'just delivered.' C. renders the line 'with mother bees and their plenteous young.'

141. **uberrima pinus**, "presumably planted for propolis, but also for pollen from the ripe male cones," Royds.

142-3. It may be best to retain the Latin order: 'and as many apples as the prolific tree had clothed itself with in its fresh blossom, no fewer did it retain when autumn was come.' There could be no *poma* while the tree was in early bloom: the slight inaccuracy of language is somewhat characteristic of V.: the blossoms are treated as the equivalent of later fruit: it is a pointed way of saying that every blossom set. (A single MS. has *legebat*.)

144. **etiam** here = 'even.' 'He was even known to plant out in rows elms of some age.' This and the next three instances imply the old gardener's consummate skill in successfully transplanting trees which were past the usual age for moving or were hard-wooded or were even old enough to bear plums or to supply shade to those sitting beneath. **versus** is said originally to mean 'a furrow,' a *vertendo aratro*, whence it comes to be used of a written line.

147. **haec**, the whole subject of gardening.

148. Columella, who was a great admirer of V., wrote his *De Re Rustica* about A.D. 50, and undertook in his tenth book, treating of horticulture, the task which V. omitted. He even tells us that V.'s words here suggested to him to write it, as he has done, in hexameter verse: *ut poeticis numeris explerem Georgici carminis omissas partes quas tamen et ipse Vergilius significaverat posteris se memorandas relinquere.*

"The number of honey and pollen-yielding blossoms mentioned at 116-148 can hardly be accidental," necessary as these are to fertilise the fruit-blossoms of cucumbers especially. "The Corycian's garden and apiary owed much of their success to their mutual relationship," Royds.

149-196

149-152. We must not miss the significance of this sentence. The marvellous skill of the bees is a special gift from Heaven. Royds refers to "a vast number of facts which tend to prove the existence of intelligence of a high order in the bee. Either she possesses something more than instinct, or she has been the object of Divine 'directivity' to an exceptional degree. The evolution of the bees has not been accomplished by mere natural selection. V. had a glimpse of the truth when he wrote of *naturas apibus quas Iuppiter ipse addidit*. The Koran, in its chapter on the bee, agrees with him: 'The Lord spake by inspiration unto the bee,'" pp. 87–8. The reward granted to the bees was that they alone of animals (*solae* ll. 153 and 155) should live in the social state. V. apparently forgets the ants.

149. **naturas**, 'the inherent qualities' or 'instincts.' **ipse**, 'of his own act.'

150. **addidit** implies that special instincts were given besides or modifying those which they already had. **pro qua mercede**, 'the recompense they gained when they followed.' This phrase is meant to emphasize not a reward as motiving an act but the greatness of the boon itself.

152. **sub**, 'deep in the cave of Dicte.' The myth was that Saturn the father of Jupiter devoured his children but that his mother hid Jupiter in a cave on Mt Dicte in Crete and that the Curetes (priests of Cybele, the Magna Mater) saved him by drowning his cries with the clash of their cymbals while the bees attracted by the noise settled there and fed the infant with their honey. Here we have a relic of the savage worship of prehistoric Greece. Gods devouring their children form no part of the beautiful Greek mythology.

153. **solae.** "The ancients knew very little of the other social insects (wasps, hornets, ants)," S. **consortia**, *consors* is usually active, 'sharer' but here passive 'shared in.' C. seems right in saying that *urbis* is the emphatic word here: the sense being they possess a city with dwellings in common.

154. **agito** here as at G. II, 157 is used =*ago*, of spending time.

155. 'They alone know the claims of country and a permanent home.' **novere**, 'recognize.'

157. 'Lay up what they have earned for the good of all.'

158. **victu**, the old contracted form of the dative, 'watch sleeplessly over the gathering of food,' and by regular compact perform their labour in the fields.' Blackmore renders *foedere pacto*, 'with time-code fixed.'

159. **saepta viarum.** This idiom is not known in early Latin and is very rare in Cicero. Lucr. however is fond of it. It is very common in later writers, especially in Tacitus. Virgil uses it frequently as in *strata viarum =vias stratas, Aen.* I, 422.

Madvig, § 284, explains it as sometimes partitive in meaning (*saeptas partes domorum*) or, as here, expressing quality, *saeptas domos*.

160. **narcissi lacrimam.** A mistake, narcissi yield pollen but not propolis. See note on l. 39.

162. **suspendunt,** 'they hang in the air.' This, says Royds, "is the right word, for bees build from the top downwards. But they have been known to build upwards when no other way was possible." "Probably V. was quite unaware that wax is a secretion of the bee. This was discovered by Huber. The wax oozes out in plates or scales from the 'wax pockets' on the under side of the abdomen."

164. **distendunt,** 'strain the cells to bursting.'

165. "Lord Avebury found the same bees doing sentry-duty day after day," Royds. **sorti,** probably an old form of the ablative.

166. **in vicem spec.,** 'they take their turn in watching for.'

168. Neither V. nor Aristotle has any suspicion that the drones are in reality the males, though Columella perhaps had some intuition of this: *Verum tamen ad procreationem subolis conferre aliquod hi fuci videntur* (IX, 15, 1). In August the drones either die of starvation or are massacred by the workers.

169. 'The work is all aglow.' V. uses the same metaphor of the toilers eagerly building their new city at Carthage, *Aen.* I, 436.

170. **Cyclopes.** In Greek mythology the Cyclopes as they appear in the *Odyssey* are one-eyed, cannibal, giant shepherds in Sicily. "The tradition is much later which makes them forgers in the huge foundry of Hephaistos (Vulcan) in the caverns of Aetna and the volcanic Liparean islands off the North of Sicily," S.

171. **properant,** 'forge in haste from the reluctant ore.'

173. **lacus,** originally a tank, or wine-vat, usually rendered here 'a trough.' C. in his translation renders it 'in the lake': in a note in his Third Edition (1872) he inclines to this rendering "as if nothing smaller than a lake or pool would suit the gigantic operations of the Cyclopes."

174. Note the cadence. Every foot suggests the regular rhythmic thud of the sledge-hammers.

175. **in numerum,** 'rhythmically,' 'ding-dong.' *In* with the accusative is used to express manner, as *in morem,* 'duly,' *in orbem,* 'in a circle.' **versant,** note the frequentative 'keep turning.'

177. **Cecropias,** 'Athenian,' a 'literary epithet' derived from

Cecrops, an early king of Attica. The honey of Hymettus, a hill near Athens, was famous. The name of Athens adds distinction. See note on I, 120.

178–180. **grandaevis oppida curae**. "This is an unfortunate after-thought. V. has fallen into the same error as Aristotle," Royds. **munire favos**, 'building walls of honeycomb.'

179. **daedala**, 'cunningly-wrought.' It is a favourite word of Lucretius who applies it to the earth as producing many various flowers or manifold crops and fruits, also in a passive sense to poems and statues. The word suggests here the varied and beautifully finished forms of the cells, adapted to their several purposes.

180. **multa nocte**. Is this correct? "Bees do not usually leave the hives after night-fall, but on light July nights may be heard working in lime-trees," Royds.

181. **thymo**. "Varro (III, 16, 11) speaks of a thyme-garden of one acre near Falerii which produced at least 10,000 sesterces (£100) a year in honey," Royds. Here and at l. 169 as also at *Ecl.* v, 77 ('as long as bees shall feed on thyme') this is regarded as the chief food-plant of the bee. Acc. to V. bees feed on the blossom of certain trees, the arbute, the willow, the lime-tree, the pine (which yields both pollen and propolis, see note on l. 39), also on the flowers of thyme (both the wild, serpyllum, l. 31, and the garden sort), savory, which is also strongly aromatic, the crocus, hyacinth, rosemary and casia (?lavender). At *Aen.* vi, 709 he speaks of their fondness for the lily. The pine-tree and thyme are of special importance: the bee-keeper must fetch plants of these from the mountains and set them all about the hives (ll. 112–13, also 181–3). See also note on 148. **pascor**, a reflexive verb with deponent force, frequent in V. who uses it actively as here. The arbute is an evergreen bush with fine foliage and scarlet fruit resembling a strawberry. It is indigenous in Britain at Killarney. **passim**, wherever the plant named grows.

182. **salices**. The willow-blossom is said to provide the earliest nectar for bees in Southern England. **casia**, an aromatic plant with leaves like the olive: cf. *G.* II, 213 *humiles casias*, where it is linked with *rorem*, 'rosemary,' as food for bees. It is strange that V. does not name lavender, which one sees growing side by side with rosemary on hills in the S. of Europe, as also one of the food-plants.

183. **pinguem tiliam**. Acc to C. *pinguem* means 'glutinous-leaved.' Mackail renders 'rich lime-blossom.' **ferrugineos** is used of objects widely differing in hue, "usually," says S.

"of any dark purple, reddish or violet colour." Its meaning depends on what flower is meant by *hyacinthos*. In *Ecl.* III, 63 V. calls this *suave rubens*, while Ovid, speaking of the transformation of Hyacinthus, a youth accidentally slain by Apollo, says *Tyrioque nitentior ostro flos oritur*. From these references Martyn and Keightley both identify it as the Martagon Lily. According to the myth the hyacinth leaf was marked with the first letter of Hyacinthus's name, or in another form of the myth by AI, AI (=αἰαῖ 'alas') as commemorating the tragic death of Ajax (Αἴας).

184. **una,** unus, 'one time of.'

185. **easdem** seems superfluous after *rursus*. V. wishes to emphasize the uniformity of their action in common.

190. **in noctem,** 'far into the night': *in* implies continuance. **sopor suus.** For the use of *suus* we may compare *Aen.* v, 832 *ferunt sua flamina classem*, of a favouring breeze: *vere suo* at l. 22 of this *Georgic*, of the spring which quickens the life of the bees. It might therefore mean here 'kindly sleep.' The elaborate comparison of bees to human beings throughout might suggest 'a sleep of their own kind.' So K. who compares *solem suum* at *Aen.* VI, 641: the spirits in Elysium have a 'sun of their own.' *Suus* is repeatedly joined with *proprius* in Livy in a sense somewhat akin to the latter meaning. **sopor,** 'deep sleep.' Note the collocation with *fessos*, 'sleep such as fatigue demands'; compare *soporatum* of the 'drugged' branch at *Aen.* v, 855. Royds says: "It is doubtful if bees ever really sleep, even in the coldest winter."

196. **tollunt.** "The spondee followed by a pause, expresses the difficulty of rising into the air so ballasted," C.

207. Acc. to V. bees do not live over seven summers. In fact "the natural term of a worker-bee's life is only six weeks," or, if born late in autumn, six months. R.

210–218

210–211. These Eastern nations were to Greeks and Romans types of despotic rule. The name of Egypt would suggest to Roman readers Cleopatra and the battle of Actium, fought in 31, about the time when V. was finishing the *Georgics*. **ingens.** Croesus' extension of his kingdom over the nations round had become proverbial. The Hydaspes is a tributary of the Indus and nearly a thousand miles away from Media proper. "However," says S., "if we take *Medus* for Persian (as it often loosely is used), and remember that the great Persian empire in its best days, reached to the Indus, the expression may be (poetically) justified."

213–214. **rupere, diripuere, solvere** might be called 'gnomic' perfects, so called because used in proverbs to express what often happens. But the perfect is also used to convey a sense of swift action. So here 'as soon as ever their king is slain, the bees destroy their combs.' C. explains in the same way *fugere* and *stravit* at I, 330 (see note), giving other instances of the same use at I, 49 and II, 81, as expressing 'instantaneous action.' The assonance of the three perfects here is so marked and peculiar that, in a poet for whom rhythm is so significant as it is for V., I feel that he means to indicate by it something more than merely what habitually occurs. Probably both uses are combined here as also at I, 330. Note the effect of the order in Latin: *ipsae* has its full force because *constructa mella* comes first. 'The honey they have themselves stored with such skill.' **crates,** 'wicker-work.' The holes in the combs suggest the comparison, 'the combs' cunning wicker-work,' C.

215. **custos,** 'the overseer.'

216. **stipo** is used of attendants or body-guards, e.g. *stipatus lictoribus,* Cic. *Verr.* II, 4, 40.

218. **per vulnera,** 'in the shower of wounds.'

219–227

219–227. The same doctrine recurs, strongly tinged with Orphism, at *Aen.* VI. 724, where it carries a distinct note of personal belief.

219. **signis,** 'from tokens like these and led by these precedents, some have asserted.' **his signis,** i.e. from such attributes as their laying up food for winter, their strict subdivision of labour, their loyalty to their king, for whom they will die in battle, in all these points resembling humanity, etc.

220. **haustus aetherios,** 'a draught of pure aether.' The aether, according to ancient philosophers, was an element akin to fire. It was lighter than the other four, and therefore Lucretius and others held that it rose to the top and surrounded the world with a fiery bastion, which he calls by a noble phrase, *flammantia moenia mundi.* Ancient thinkers generally held the aether to be of the same substance with the human mind: it was also identified with the human mind and with the *anima mundi* or 'world-spirit.'

In this passage, ll. 219–227, V. blends two doctrines; the first being that bees have more than other creatures been inspired with wisdom by the Gods: thus Aristotle in *De Generat. Anim.*

III, 10, says that they have θεῖόν τι, 'some divine quality.' The strange practice of 'telling the bees,' i.e. of informing them of the death of the master of the house and garden, which, accompanied with various ceremonies, used to be common all over England, implies in them a degree of intelligence and as it were human feeling which men impute to almost no other creature. The second doctrine is that there is a world-spirit which pervades all things and is the source of all life. This is more fully stated at *Aen.* VI, 724, where he says that heaven and earth, sea and sun and moon 'are kept alive by a spirit within them, and Mind pervading the members stirs the whole frame of the world and mingles with the mighty mass.' Here we have the Stoic notion of an Anima Mundi, also held by the Platonists. V. was greatly influenced by Epicureanism while writing the *Georgics*, but he was even more of a Lucretian than an Epicurean and held his mind open to other doctrines. The Epicureans held that the soul was in the main akin to the aether but they strenuously denied the existence of any Anima Mundi.

As to the indwelling of Mind in animals a very able biologist and thinker, Dr J. A. Hadfield, refers to the theory of a "cosmic mind" (passive and impersonal when manifested in the lowest forms of life) "which dwells in all living things and works out its purposes in them." See his paper "Mind and Brain," in the volume entitled *Immortality*, ed. by B. H. Streeter, Macmillan, 1917.

221. **ire,** 'for a God they tell us pervades all lands.'

222. **terrasque.** Note the lengthening of *que* usually before liquids or double consonants when the ictus falls upon it.

223. 'From Him, flocks, herds,' etc. **pecus, pecudis** means smaller cattle especially sheep; **armentum,** from *arare*, cattle employed in ploughing.

224. **tenues vitas,** 'its subtle essence of life.'

225. **scilicet huc,** 'to him again all things thereafter are restored and return,' *scilicet*, continuing the explanation, 'further,' 'again.'

Note also the assonance of *reddi, resoluta, referri*: the accumulated expression is meant to emphasize the doctrine that no life perishes, though the body is broken up into its elements.

226. **nec morti esse locum.** Compare the pantheistic faith of Emily Brontë's last verses: "Though earth and men were gone....Every existence would exist in Thee. There is no room for death, Nor atom that his might could render void."

227. **sideris in numerum.** The use of *sideris* in the singular is strange and might seem an echo of Lucr. I, 436 *corporis*

augebil numerum where *corpus* is used in its abstract sense. It has been explained by taking *sidus* as a noun of multitude, cf. *glandis*, for 'acorns' at *G.* 1, 8. But C. seems right in comparing it with phrases, such as *in numero esse*, 'to have a share' in a thing as at Lucr. v, 180: cf. *in hostium numero habere aliquem*, 'to reckon a man among one's enemies,' Caes. *B.G.* 1, 28: *tibi parentis numero esse*, Cic. *Div. in Caec.* XIX, 61. See Munro's note on Lucr. v, 51. C. renders 'into the ranks of the stars.'

453-470

There is reason to believe that V. omitted the original latter half of *G.* IV, and substituted for it the story of Aristaeus. Acc. to Suetonius the closing part of *G.* IV. dealt with the career of Gallus, Virgil's fellow-student and the intimate friend of his early manhood. Gallus, born in very humble position, rose to eminence both as soldier and poet and became the first viceroy of Egypt. In this high office he offended Augustus by his ambition and, losing all hope of appeasing him, took his own life at the age of 43. The emperor resented V.'s choice of such a subject and the poet felt compelled to cut it out. Much has thus been lost to us in the picture of a striking personality who was both V.'s comrade and the partner of his poetic efforts. Princely patronage has its own dangers for the poet no less than Grub Street. See also *Addenda.*

Aristaeus is a bee-keeper who has lost by disease the whole stock of the hives in which he takes pride. Falling back on the poetic machinery of the *Odyssey*, V. represents him as resorting to the sea-deity, Proteus, who has prophetic power, in order to learn the cause of his distress.

Like Ulysses Aristaeus must first of all bind Proteus or he will give him no counsel. When thus handled, Proteus reveals the cause of the loss of his bees. While Eurydice, the wife of Orpheus, was fleeing from Aristaeus who was pursuing her in mad passion along the river, she set foot on a huge water-snake whose bite caused her death. It is because of this wrong that Divine vengeance is pursuing him. The Dryads or Tree Spirits, of whom Eurydice was one, have sent the plague on his bees. When the cause is thus learned, Aristaeus appeases the Dryads and the spirit of Orpheus by sacrifices. He is told to leave the bodies of the victims lying in the grove and to revisit the spot on the ninth day. When he does this he finds the carcasses humming with bees.

453. 'No!—think not that 'tis aught lesser than a God

whose anger now harasses thee: the crime thou art suffering
for is a great one.' **nullius**. Note the short accented final
syllable lengthened.

455. **ob meritum**. These words, if correct, cannot apply to
Aristaeus' offence, but to the undeserved sorrow of Orpheus,
"a wretched man by no fault of his own," C., but the order of
the words does not harmonize with this. The emphatic place
of *tibi* and the conjunction of *poenas* with *meritum* confirm the
reading of the Palatine MS. *ad meritum*, 'punishment by no
means in proportion to your crime,' i.e. far milder. S. following
Servius interprets *ob meritum* in the latter sense, by a great
strain on language.

457. **illa...puella**. C. sees here an instance of what may
be called the pronominal use of the article or rather of the
pronoun before it grew into the article. He adds: "Note the
delicacy with which V. instead of mentioning Eurydice's death
intimates it by the single word *moritura*." **dum te fugeret**. A
unique use because there is no verb for the *dum* clause to depend on as at *Aen*. I, 5. S. says: "The real help to the analysis
is given by the word *praeceps*." He suggests "that the fuller
sense, *dum praeceps currebat ut te fugeret* is compressed into
dum te fugeret praeceps." At the same time V., as his way often
is, seems to have in his mind a second construction, viz. *dum* =
dummodo, 'if only she might escape,' 'in her hurry to escape.'
See Lewis Campbell's *Sophocles*, vol. I, 2nd edition, 1879, p. 66,
on "Double Constructions." **per** extended to mean 'along,' as
at *Aen*. V, 662.

460. **aequalis**, 'of her own years.' **supremos montes**, so loud
was the cry. Is there here an unconscious memory of the
'marvellous wailing that arose over the ocean' from Thetis
and her sea-nymphs when the body of her son Achilles was
being washed before the funeral-rites; a cry so terrible that the
awe-struck Greeks wished to retire to their ships? (*Od.*
XXIV, 47.)

461–3. **Rhodopeïae**, the diphthong is shortened, when
not in arsis, before a word beginning with a vowel as at
Aen. III, 211 *insulae Ionio*. **implerunt, flerunt**. The rhyme
is here intentional and suggests the haunting repetition of
sorrowful thought, perhaps, as Winbolt says, the echo of
the Dryads' wail in the mountains. The same mournful itera-
tion is found at l. 466 *te veniente die, te decedente, canebat*, and
also at l. 509. **Rhodope** and **Pangaea** are mountain-ranges, one
in Thrace, the other in Macedonia. **Hebrus** is the chief river
in Thrace. **Orithyia**, daughter of Erechtheus, King of Attica,

was carried off by Boreas to Thrace. The old name of Attica was 'Actaea' from *acte*, 'the beach' (from which is borrowed the Latin *acta*, *Aen.* v, 613).

467. **Taenarias fauces**. At Taenarus (Cape Matapan) there was a cave supposed to lead to the infernal regions.

468. 'The grove shrouding itself in black terror.' Groves were regarded with awe as the abode of spirits: they fill the region between earth and Hades and surround the Styx. See *Aen.* VI, 131 *tenent media omnia silvae*, also 154, 238. Note the succession of spondees marking grimness as it does sorrow in 465.

471–503

471. **commotae**, 'startled.'

472. **ibant**, 'came trooping.' **simulacraque luce carentum**, from Lucr. IV, 35 (of phantoms seen in dreams). The expression is Lucretian in its vividness. It is far more in keeping here than at l. 255, of the dead bees. It recalls Browning: "Death stepped tacitly and took them where they never see the sun" (*A Toccata of Galuppi's*).

474. 'When roosting or when a winter rain-storm brings them down from the mountains.' **vesper** is construed with *agit* only.

475–477 are repeated at *Aen.* VI, 306–8. They are suggested by *Od.* XI, 38: Ulysses sacrifices before his descent into hell and the spirits gather to the blood, including many slain in battle. **corpora**, not a confusion between the dead body and the spirit. The spirits reproduce in aspect the stately figures of the living heroes. Cf. *Aen.* II, 18 *delecta virum corpora*, 'of the heroes in the horse.'

476. **magnanimûm**. Dr Fowler says: "For me the meaning is rather what I may call 'eugenic' than simply ethical: it is the word for heroes (here and at *Aen.* VI, 649), men lifted above the ordinary level of humanity by descent and therefore, as the old idea of breeding held, chivalrous and great-hearted" (*Death of Turnus*, p. 152).

478. **deformis**, 'loathly.'

479, 480. **Cocytus**, the river of wailing: **Styx**, the hateful river: **palus** is of course the slow, stagnant Styx. **interfusa** refers to *quos* l. 478. 'Wound nine times round them,' C.: the Styx is supposed to enclose parts of Erebus between each fold. The rivers of the lower world are not bright, swift-running streams but sluggish and stagnant, like marshes. Newman's lines are true to Pagan feeling, "The low beach and silent gloom, And chilling mists of that dull river, Along whose bank the thin ghosts shiver, The thin, wan ghosts that once were men" (*Callista*, Chapter x).

481. 'Nay, the very home of death was astounded.' C. renders 'a charm fell on the very,' etc. **ipsae** includes the place and the Furies and Cerberus too.

482. **Tartarus** is the lowest abyss of hell: see *Aen.* vi, 577.

484. **Ixion**, king of the Lapithae in Thessaly, was bound fast to a wheel in Tartarus as punishment for his crimes. **rota orbis**, 'the circle of the wheel,' for *orbis rotae*. **vento**, 'the wind fell,' abl. of the instrument: condensed for 'from lack of wind.' See C. on *Ecl.* ii, 26, *cum placidum ventis staret mare*.

487. **hanc legem**, 'this condition,' same as *foedera* at l. 493, namely that Orpheus should not look back till both had reached the upper air.

489. **Manes**, properly the shades but here ='the Powers below,' Pluto and Proserpina.

490–2. **Eurydicenque suam**, "E. was now his own, treading on the very threshold of daylight," C., "when alas! he forgot, and no longer master of himself he looked back. That instant all his toil was spilt like water." **animi** is the locative case. **victus**, 'overpowered by passion.' Note the effect of the sudden check in the metre and sense after *respexit*. The four brief words which follow are thus made to emphasize the sudden transformation wrought by Orpheus' error.

493. **foedera**, 'the covenant.' **fragor**, 'a thunder-crash.' This reminds us of the appalling effectiveness of the subterranean thunder, which accompanies the passing of Oedipus in Sophocles' play.

495. 'Woe is me! what madness, what monstrous madness has destroyed both me and thee?' I cannot agree with Mackail in rendering, 'Who hath destroyed me?' etc. The repeated *quis* is inconsistent with this meaning. **retro** is used vaguely but effectively. The Fates were not calling E. back 'a second time.'

496. 'Swimming eyes' suggests to us weeping. But here it denotes dim and flickering sight, so used at *Aen.* v, 856 of the pilot's eyes overpowered by sleep.

497. 'The vast night closes round me and I am borne away.' **nocte**. A minute before they were just emerging into daylight.

500. **fugit diversa**, 'she vanished right away from him.' **diversa** means 'in the opposite direction,' here almost ='back-

wards.' **tenues** qualifies *auras*: the air is as unsubstantial as the disembodied spirit.

501. **umbras**, not a poetic plural denoting the spirit of E.: Orpheus clutches at the darkness which has swallowed her up, but in which he yet strives to grasp her.

502. **praeterea**, 'any longer': so at *Aen.* I, 49 *et quisquam nomen Iunonis adorat Praeterea?*

503. **obiectam paludem**, 'the barrier of marsh,' i.e. Styx.

504–527

505. Blackmore renders: 'All moans, all music were but waste of breath.' **manes**, in same sense as at l. 489, includes, acc. to C., "the Powers below as well as the shades subject to them." In this line may not *numina movere* mean 'to bend the decrees' of those deities? the old Italian conception of *Numen* being, as Dr Fowler has shown, a manifestation of will-power rather than a personal deity, *R.E.R.*, p. 118. Thus at *Aen.* VIII, 574 *numina vestra*, addressed to Jupiter, means 'Thy august will.' Or does Orpheus in his frenzy forget that the Gods of the upper world have no jurisdiction here?

506. **nabat**. Cf. the German colloquial *Er schwimmt*, 'He is on a voyage.'

509. **evolvisse**, probably a metaphor from unrolling a book.

511. **populea sub umbra**. In his *Year with the Birds*, Dr Warde Fowler says that this, the single passage in which V. mentions the nightingale, is inferior in truth to Homer's lines on which it is based. V. has chosen the most thinly-leaved of all trees, whereas its habit is to sing amidst thick cover, nor does he refer to the variety of its song. Homer (*Od.* XIX, 518) truthfully describes the bird as 'singing from amid the thick leafage of the trees and pouring forth her many-toned music with many a varied turn.' But he now holds that the poet was, after all, perfectly true to nature. He actually heard the bird singing *populea sub umbra*. It was perched on the lower branch of a tall Lombardy poplar, which grew out of a thick undergrowth of willow, alder, etc., in which no doubt the nest was.....The ploughman discovers the nest in the scrub and the bird retires to a poplar branch to give voice to its grief (*Class. Rev.* for 1890, p. 49). By an oversight the former opinion stands repeated in a later edition of the book (1902). But Dr Fowler writes me that his opinion of 1890 is unchanged, and that the bird does, on occasion, sing in the open.

513. **observans,** 'has marked.' "The word is used loosely, to supply the want of an aorist participle, the sense being 'observatos detraxit,'" C. Note the pause after *detraxit* which calls attention back to the bird.

516. **Venus,** 'love.' **flexere,** 'had power over.'

517, 518. The **Hyperboreans,** a fabulous people whom Homer conceives as living 'beyond the North Wind': the term came to mean simply 'most northerly.' **Tanais,** the river Don in central Russia. **Rhipaeis,** giant mountains believed to separate the Hyperboreans from the rest of the world: the Urals probably gave rise to the legend.

519. Note the emphatic position of *raptam* and *irrita.*

520. The **Cicones** were a Thracian tribe near the mouth of the Hebrus. **munus** means 'a service,' and is specially used of funeral honours; 'slighted by such devotion,' i.e. by his undying constancy to Eurydice.

521. **orgia,** 'revels.'

523. **tum quoque,** 'even then.'

524. **Oeagrus** was King of Thrace and father ot Orpheus.

525. **vox ipsa,** 'his voice of itself,' i.e. even though life had fled.

526. 'Kept calling with his last fleeting breath.'

527. **toto flumine,** 'all down the stream,' a local ablative like *caelo* in *G.* 1, 6 where see note.

559–566

559. **haec canebam,** 'such is the song I was making on the tending of fields and cattle.' "*Canebam* is probably the common imperfect as used in correspondence," says C., "referring to the time when a letter is read not when it was written," and it thus suggests that the successes of Caesar were still going on when the *Georgics* were finished.

560–1. **Caesar magnus,** 'Caesar the great,' as if conferring a title upon him. After the victory at Actium in 31 B.C. Augustus marched triumphantly through Syria and Asia Minor. But there was no fighting. Hence **fulminat bello** is here an exaggeration. **Victor** and **volentes** qualify each other, 'a welcome conqueror.' The phrase **iura dare,** 'to dispense laws,' occurs in Horace, *Odes* III, 3 *triumphatis dare iura Medis,* but the context is very different. In *volentes* V. claims for Augustus that his world-empire is no mere reign of brute force but that his justice secures the allegiance of his subjects.

562. **affectat** "almost =*ingreditur,*" C. 'Essays the path to heaven'; is working his way to immortality and godship.

Olympo, poetic use for *ad Olympum*, cf. *facilis descensus Averno, Aen.* VI, 126. After Augustus had settled affairs in Parthia, it was decreed that his name should be included along with those of the Gods in the public forms of religious service. Dio 51, c. 20.

563. 'I, V., was being nurtured in the lap of sweet Parthenope, delighting in the pursuits of inglorious ease.'

564. **florentem,** lit. 'blossoming,' often used to express the high-tide of youth, the 'Blüthezeit' or blossoming-time. But Cicero, writing to the philosopher, Nigidius Figulus (*Ep.* IV, 13), has *studia, artes quibus a pueritia floruisti.* On the use of *floreo* in Virgil see Fowler's interesting note (*Gathering of the Clans,* p. 87).

564. **Parthenope.** Naples, so named after a Siren believed to have been buried there.

565. **audax iuventa,** because he was the first to imitate Theocritus by writing Idylls in Latin.

lusi, 'who once played with shepherds' songs.' *Ludo* = to do anything in sport or for pastime. The term is here highly significant, V. employs it repeatedly in speaking of his own early poetry (at *Ecl.* I, 10; VI, 1; VII, 17). By using it again he intends us to know that he regarded his *Eclogues,* however perfect of their kind, as a work of his youth, something which he had outgrown.

The writer of the *Georgics* and *Aeneid* (the latter no doubt already planned and half-completed) must have felt that the setting of the *Eclogues,* presenting all classes of men as shepherds, was artificial and a fashion of the time. These closing words indicate the spirit of the poet, who disowned his own early writings, who was always striving after higher achievement. The thunders of war waged by the great Ruler of Rome have made themselves heard amid his silvan quiet. V. too feels himself bound to a greater task than before for his country's sake. These closing lines seem to breathe the noble ambition which Virgil, speaking in his own name, seems to transfer to his hero when, after the sacramental meeting with his father's spirit, Aeneas rises with enlargement of soul and devotion to a full acceptance of the duties of his career—

maior rerum mihi nascitur ordo[1].

---

[1] *Aen.* VII, 44. In a chapter on "Religious Feeling in Virgil," Dr W. Fowler has subtly and convincingly traced the development of the character of Aeneas, as he rises in the course of the story into the heroic type, the turning-point of the change being the interview with Anchises in Hades. *R.E.R.* Lecture XVIII.

ADDENDA

1. Preface, pp. vii–viii. Conington's success as a translator must not be estimated from his verse-rendering of the *Aeneid*. It is almost inexplicable that one whom Henry calls truly "a scholar at once and a poet" should have chosen for this a metre so repugnant to the genius of Virgil's majestic, yet pliant hexameter as is that of *Marmion* and the *Lady of the Lake* with its peculiar rhythm and assonance, its monotonous and incessant rhymes. Our loss is the greater because hardly another man has united in himself in equal degree the intimate mastery of Virgil's most subtle style, the love and reverence for the poet along with the easy command of verse, all of which are necessary in order to reproduce for English readers what Douglas calls

> The beauty of his ornate eloquence.

"I have read Conington's translation from beginning to end with endless admiration of his extraordinary prosodic skill but with ever-increasing regret that he adopted a metre, which is quite incapable of rendering or suggesting

> The stateliest measure ever moulded by the lips of man.

Yet, even as it stands, it seems to me that there are passages which, in spite of the cramped scope of the verse, could hardly be bettered in combined felicity of phrase and fidelity of rendering." H. A. W.

2. Introduction, p. xxxvi (foot) add:

Thus at *G.* II, 149 V. says that in Italy (meaning in certain districts) sheep breed and fruit-trees bear twice a year. It never occurs to him to enquire how such facts stand related, whether as exceptions or as seeming contradictions to the great doctrine of Law in Nature which governs Lucretius's outlook, according to which "we see each thing produced afresh and well-defined periods fixed for things, each after its kind, to reach the flower of their age" (Lucr. I, 562–4). See note on *G.* II, 149.

3. *G.* IV, 37. There is no foundation for the usual assertion that Xenophon speaks of "a Queen-bee" at *Oecon.* VII, 17, ἡ ἡγεμὼν μέλιττα, literally "the leader-bee," the article here being feminine. But in two other passages, *Cyrop.* V, I. 24, and *Hell.* III, 2. 28, he uses the same two words along with the masculine article. Remembering that μέλιττα, like *apis*

in Latin, has only one gender, feminine, no such inference can be drawn.

4. *G.* IV, 182, *glaucas salices.* Martyn in his edition of the *Georgics,* 1746, seems to give the exact force of *glaucus* here. Commenting on *G.* II, 13:

> Glaucâ canentia fronde salicta,

he says, "This is a beautiful description of the common willow: the leaves are of a bluish-green and the under-side of them is covered with a white down."

5. Note on IV, 220. With regard to the theory of a "cosmic mind," referred to by Dr Hadfield, a sentence of Aristotle deserves to be quoted:

"Perhaps even in the lower creatures there is some natural principle of good, superior to their own instincts, which strives after the good that is proper for them." *Nicom. Ethics,* X, 2. 4.

6. *G.* IV. 453. Servius (whose commentary on Virgil dates from the fourth century, but is based on far older sources) asserts that the poet substituted the story of Orpheus for his encomium on Gallus at the command of Augustus. This statement used to be suspected as without foundation, but a discovery made in 1896 confirms its truth. An inscribed stone was then found in the paved approach to the ruined temple of Augustus at Philae in Egypt, which was built in B.C. 12. The inscription records the victories of Gallus in Latin, Greek and Egyptian, the Latin one being the fullest. In this Gallus describes himself as "the subduer of the whole Thebaid region in fifteen days," as "having carried his armies above the cataract of the Nile to a spot never before reached by the Roman people," as having taken cities and so on, while Augustus is only named in the beginning as "having conquered the kings of Egypt," that is Cleopatra and, probably, Antony. A portrait in the centre of the inscription represents a Roman knight riding down a suppliant foe, but "the features have been deliberately hacked out for the same reason which induced the builders of the temple to place the slab with the inscription face upwards to be trodden underfoot...viz. to do dishonour to Gallus." See Prof. R. S. Conway's book, most valuable to students of Virgil, *New Studies of a great Inheritance,* 1921, pp. 105–11.

The provocation given by Gallus' vanity was extreme, but we need not suppose Augustus' interference in the poem to be prompted by mere resentment. We are told that, on hearing of the death of Gallus, he burst into tears, exclaiming that "he was the only man on earth not allowed to be angry with a friend if he chose," that is, to be angry without being punished for it. These are the words of true and bitter regret. It was not unnatural that the Emperor should not wish a story so tragic, in which he had himself borne a part, to be handed down by Rome's greatest poet.

7. *G.* IV, 505. It should be noted that MSS. Rom. and Med. read *quae* for *qua*.

8. Sargeaunt's *Trees, Shrubs and Plants of Virgil* (Blackwell, 1920), which has just reached me, gives a botanist's careful observations, made while residing in Italy. The writer identifies *casia* of *G.* IV, 30 with the Spurge Laurel which is akin to the Daphne Mezereon. *Apium*, he says, is not parsley but celery. Virgil's poppy seems to have been the opium-poppy, the seeds of which are not narcotic. The pine of the old Corycian's garden, which V. advises the bee-keeper to transplant from the high hills (*G.* IV, 112), is our own Scotch pine which is chiefly an Alpine.

It must be remembered that the precision of poetry is not always that of prose. Yet V. can be precise enough, as in the description of *amellus* in *G.* IV, 271 ff. which could not be more clear than it is. The lovely picture of a fruit-tree in full blossom at *G.* I, 186–7 is identified by one botanist with the walnut, by another with the almond. This is puzzling. Here perhaps the poet drew from a mental picture which united details gathered from various fruit-trees in the beauty and fragrance of their flower. The name 'hyacinth' has evidently been applied to widely differing plants in different times and places. In such cases poets, who often tend to draw from books rather than from nature, may amalgamate features of various plants and thus produce a poetic hybrid which no botanist can identify.

Dr Warde Fowler's Gifford Lectures on Roman religion are referred to as *R.E.R.* Pap. stands for Papillon's edition of the *Georgics*, K. for that of Keightley, H. for the fifth edition of Conington's commentary, revised by Haverfield, Vol. I, 1898, R. for Royds' *Beasts, Birds and Bees of Virgil*.

VOCABULARY

*(The words commonest in Caesar and Ovid
are not included.)*

abies, -etis, f. *the silver fir.*

abiungo, -ĕre, -nxi, -nctum, *unyoke.*

abstrudo, -ĕre, -si, -sum, *thrust away, hide.*

acanthus, -i, m., (1) an Eastern tree, *the acacia* (see n., II, 119); (2) at IV, 123, a plant, *the bear's foot* (named from shape of leaves. The word means 'thorn-flower' from Gk *ake*, a pointed thing, and *anthos*, flower).

acer, -cris, -cre, *sharp, spirited.*

acervus, -i, m. *heap.*

acies, -ei, f. *sharp edge, line of battle.*

aconitum, -i, n. *wolf's-bane.*

Actias, -adis, adj. *Athenian* (Gk *akte*, coast-land, the old name of Attica).

adeo, *indeed, especially* (emphasizing the preceding word).

aditus, -us, m. *approach.*

adnuo, -ĕre, -ui, -utum, *to assent to.*

adolesco, -ĕre, -evi, -ultum, *grow up.*

adsiduus, -a, -um, *sitting fast, perpetual* (*ad, sedeo*).

aedes, -is, f. sing. *temple*; plur. generally a house containing several apartments.

aequalis, -e, *of the same age, comrade.*

aequor, -oris, n. *a level surface*, whether sea or plain (*aequus*).

aerius, -a, -um, *dropping from the air, towering.*

aestivus, -a, -um, *of summer* (*aestas*).

aestus, -us, m., (1) *a waving motion*; (2) *heat*; (3) *heaving of the sea, tide.*

aether, -eris, m. *the upper air*; personified 'the Sky.'

aevum, -i, n., (1) *eternity*; (2) *lifetime* (Gr. *aeōn*, a long period).

affecto, 1, *strive after, aspire to.*

agito, (1) *to put in motion, toss*; (2) (of time) *to spend* (freq. from *ago*, as if from a supine, *agitu*).

agmen, -inis, n., (1) *any thing or body of things in motion*; (2) *a column on the march.*

agrestis, -e, *belonging to the fields*: subs. *a country-man.*

albesco, -ĕre, *to grow white.*

alienus, -a, -um, *belonging to another.*

almus, -a, -um (from *alo*), *bountiful, kindly.*

alnus, -i, f. *alder-tree.*

alternis, *alternately* (abl. neut. of *alternus*, -a, -um).

altus, -a, -um, *high, deep*: **altum**, as subs. *the deep.*

alvare, -is, n. *a bee-hive* (*alvus*, bee-hive).

alveus, -i, m. *a hollow vessel, trough, channel of river.*

ambages, -is, f. *a going round about.*

amnis, -is, m., (1) *a great river* (contrasted with *flumen*); (2) *a stream.*

amurga, -ae, f. *fluid pressed from olives; lees of oil.*

angustus, -a, -um, *narrow.*

anima, -ae, f. *a breeze, breath, life, soul* (Gk *anemos,* the wind).

anser, -eris, m. *goose* (root of *gander,* German *Gans*).

antiquus, -a, -um, *ancient, olden* (of what has passed away: *vetus* =old and still existing).

apis, -is, f. *a bee.*

apium, -ii, n. *parsley.*

appareo, 2, *to be clearly seen* (see n. on 1, 404).

apricus, -a, -um, *open to the sun, basking in the sun* (*aperio*).

apto, 1, *to fit, adjust* (of putting on arms).

Aquilo, -onis, m. *the North Wind.*

aquor, 1, def. *fetch water.*

Arabs, -is, c. *an Arabian.*

arbutum, -i, n. the fruit of the arbutus or strawberry tree.

arcesso, -ĕre, -ivi, -itum, *fetch, derive.*

Arctos, -i, f. the constellation of the Great and Lesser Bear.

ardea, -ae, f. *heron.*

arduus,-a,-um, *lofty, prancing*: **ardua,** n. pl. used as noun, *heights.*

area, -ae, f. *a threshing-floor.*

argutus, -a, -um, *shrill, creaking, finely-shaped* (see n. on 1, 143).

armentum, -i, n. *a herd, cattle used for ploughing, bullocks* or *horses* (from *aro*).

armus, -i, m. *shoulder.*

ars, artis, f. skill acquired in any field, scientific method, (in morals) a man's character, qualities.

arundo, -inis, f. *reed.*

arvum, -i, n. (sc. *solum*) *ploughed land, fields* (*arvus,* adj. ploughed), *pasture.*

ater, -tra, -trum, *black* (see n. on 1, 129).

atrox, -ocis, *fierce.*

attero, -ĕre, -trivi, -tritum, *wear away, bruise.*

auctor, -oris, m. *originator, adviser.*

aula, -ae, f. *court* of a house but esp. of a royal palace.

aura, -ae, f. *air, breeze.*

auritus, -a, -um, *long-eared* (*auris*).

Auster, -tri, m. *the South Wind.*

avena, -ae, f. *wild oats.*

avernus, -a, -um, *without birds* because of deadly exhalations, also with *Lacus,* or as subst. **Avernus,** -i, m. a certain lake near Cumae: hence an adj. *Avernian.*

avius, -a, -um, *pathless.*

baca, -ae, f. *berry.*

Balearis, -e, belonging to the Balearic islands which were famous for their slingers.

balo, 1, *bleat*: **balantes** as subst., *sheep.*

balsamum, -i, n. *the gum of the balsam-tree.*

bibo, -ēre, -i, -itum, *to drink.*

bicornis, -e, *two-pronged.*

bifer, -era, -erum, *bearing twice a year.*

bini, -ae, -a, *two-fold.*

Boreas, -ae, m. *the North wind.*

bracchium, -i, n. *arm, branch of tree.*

bucula, -ae, f. *heifer*

caducus, -a, -um, *falling, fallen.*

caecus, -a, -um, (1) *blind*; (2) *unseen, unknown.*

caenum, -i, n. *mud.*

Caesar, -aris, m. the name of a patrician family, applied by Virgil to Julius Caesar, I, 466, also to Augustus, IV, 560.

calamus, -i, m. *reed, stalk.*

caligo, I, *to be dark, gloomy* (*caligo*, -inis, n. denotes greater darkness than *tenebrae*).

cancer, -cri, m. *crab.*

caneo, ēre, -ui, 2, *to be grey or white.*

canorus, -a, -um, *tuneful.*

capillus, -i, m. *hair* (generally of the head).

capto, I, *to try to seize, catch at, sniff up* (frequent. *capio*).

carcer, -eris, m. *prison, starting-place in the racecourse.*

carduus, -i, m. *thistle.*

careo, 2, v. n. *to be without.*

carina, -ae, f. *keel.*

carmen, -inis, n. *a song, poetry, the charm of poetry.*

casia, -ae, f. *a herb, drug.*

castanea, -ae, f. *chestnut tree.*

cavea, -ae, f. *hollow place, hive.*

Ceres, Cereris, f., (1) the goddess of agriculture, named in Greek *Demeter* (the 'Earth-goddess'); (2) *corn.*

cerintha, -ae, f. *honey-wort.*

cesso, I, *to be idle, lie fallow.*

circumvector, I, dep. *to sail or travel round.*

clarus, -a, -um, (1) *bright* (to the eye); (2) *clear* (of sound); (3) *famous.*

classicum, -i, n. *war-trumpet.*

claustrum, -i, n. *barrier.*

coeptum, -i, n. *a beginning, attempt.*

cogo, -ĕre, coegi, coactum, *drive together, make solid, freeze.*

colludo, -ĕre, -si, -sum, *to play together.*

collum, -i, n. *the neck.*

colonus, -i, m. *tiller of soil* (*colo*).

colubra, -ae, f. *serpent.*

columna, -ae, f. *a column.*

coma, -ae, f., (1) *hair of the head*; (2) by a common but artificial metaphor *foliage.*

cometes, -ae, m. *comet* (Gk *kometes*, long-haired).

committo, -ĕre, -isi, -issum, (1) *join together*; (2) *join battle*; (3) *commit* a crime.

commoveo, -ēre, -movi, -motum, *rouse, startle.*

compesco, -ĕre, -ui, *fasten together, curb, prune* (*compes*, fetter).

compono, -ĕre, -posui, -positum, *lay together, compose* (of the limbs in attitude for sleep).

concresco, -ĕre, -crevi, -cretum, *to grow together, stiffen.*

condo, -ĕre, -didi, -ditum, *to put together, hide*: se condere, *to nestle.*

conflo, I, *blow together* (of fire), *smelt.*

congero, -ĕre, -gessi, -gestum, *pile together.*

consero, -ĕre, -sevi, -situm, *to plant.*

consido, -ĕre, -sedi, -sessum, *sink down.*

consors, -ortis, *shared, in partnership.*

contineo, 2, *to keep in.*

continuo, adv. (of one incident immediately following another), *immediately* (see n. on I, 356).

coquo, -ĕre, coxi, coctum, *cook*, (passive) *ripen.*

cor, -dis, n. (1) *the heart*; (2) *intellect*, '*wits*.'

corono, 1, *crown with a garland*.

cortex, -icis, m. and f. *bark*, esp. that of the cork-tree.

corusco, 1, *move quickly, flash*.

corylus, -i, f. *hazel-tree*.

costa, -ae, f. *a rib*.

cothurnus, -i, m. *a hunting-boot*.

crassus, -a, -um, *thick*.

crater, -eris, m. *a mixing-bow for wine*.

cratis, -is, f. *wicker-work*.

crinis, -is, m. *hair of the head*.

cruentus, -a, -um, *bloody, blood-red*.

cruor, -oris, m. *blood from a wound* (*sanguis* mainly of blood circulating in the veins).

cucumis, -eris, m. *cucumber*.

culmen, -inis, n. *top of anything, roof, tower*.

culmus, -i, m. *stalk*.

cultum, -i, n. *cultivated field* (neut. of partic. of *colo*).

cultus, -us, m. *cultivation, care*.

cumba, -ae, f. *boat*.

cunabula, -orum, n. pl. *cradle*, (*cunae*).

cuneus, -i, m. *wedge*.

cymbalum, -i, n. *cymbal*.

daedalus, -a, -um, *cunningly-wrought* (from Daedalus, builder of the Cretan labyrinth).

damma, -ae, f. *fallow-deer*.

(daps) dapis, f. *feast* (usually in plural).

decoquo, -ĕre, -xi, -ctum, *boil down*.

decurro, -ĕre, -rsi, -rsum, *run through, traverse*.

decutio, -ĕre, -cussi, -cussum, *to shake off* (*de, quatio*).

deficio, -ĕre, -feci, -fectum, *to be wanting, fail*.

deformis, -e, *unsightly, loathly*.

defungor, -i, -functus, dep. *discharge to the full, be done with*.

dehisco, -ĕre, -hivi, *gape, yawn apart*.

denseo, 2, v. a. *make thick, condense*.

depecto, -ĕre, -xi, -xum, *comb down* or *off*.

desertus, -a, -um, *waste, uninhabited*; pl. n. as noun.

desidia, -ae, f. *sloth*.

de-spumo, 1, *skim off* (*spuma*, froth, foam of the sea).

deterior, -us, n. *inferior* (positive form not found).

deveho, -ĕre, -xi, -ctum, *carry down*.

deverto, -ĕre, -ti, -sum, *turn aside*.

digero, -ĕre, -gessi, -gestum, *separate, plant out*.

dilectus, -us, m. *choice*.

dirus, -a, -um, *fearful, threatening danger, ominous*.

diversus, -a, -um, *in an opposite direction*.

divinitus, adv. *by divine influence*.

do, dare, dedi, datum, *give, put* (*dare se*, yield themselves, submit to be performed).

dulcedo, -inis, f. *sweetness, delight*.

dumus, -i, m. *bush, thorn*.

ebenus, -i, f. *the ebony tree*.

eburnus, -a, -um, *of ivory*.

e-durus, -a, -um, *exceedingly hard* (*e, ex*, intensive).

effervo, -ĕre, *boil over*.

effetus, -a, -um, *exhausted, worn out with bearing*.

effodio, -ĕre, -fodi, -fossum, *dig out*.

egestas, -atis, f. *extreme poverty, want* (much stronger than *paupertas*, which is simply 'narrow means').

electrum, -i, n., (1) *amber*; (2) *a metal* (see n. on III, 522).

elephantus, -i, m. *an elephant, ivory*.

eluceo, -ēre, -luxi, *shine out*.

enodis, -e, *without knots*.

Eous, -a, -um, *belonging to the East, in the morning*: as subst. at I, 288, *the morning star* (Gk *Eos*, the dawn).

e-quidem, *indeed* (used often by Virgil with first person as if derived from *ego*, but also with 2nd and 3rd).

Erebus, -i, m., (1) *God of Darkness*; (2) *the Lower World*.

eruo, -ēre, -ui, -utum, *root up*.

esca, -ae, f. *food* (*esco* from *edo*).

esset (at I, 151) from *edo*.

etiam-num (more often *etiam-nunc*), *still, even then*.

Eumenides, -um, f. *the Furies* (lit. 'the kindly Goddesses,' a title meant to avert their anger: so in Gaelic one designation for the Fairies is the "Men of Peace").

Eurus, -i, m. *the East wind*.

everto, -ēre, -ti, -sum, *overturn*.

exacuo, -ēre, -ui, -utum, *sharpen*.

examen, -inis, n. (for *exagmen*), *swarm*.

exaudio, 4, *to hear distinctly* (in cases where hearing is difficult or important).

exedo, -ĕre, -edi, -esum, *eat out*.

exemplum, -i, n., (1) *portrait*; (2) *instance, precedent* (*ex-*

imo, to pick out as indicative of some point).

exerceo, 2, *keep busy*: perf. part. *kept in motion, fresh*.

exesus, -a, -um, *hollow*.

exiguus, -a, -um, *scanty* (opposed to *amplus*).

exorsa, n. plur. (from perf. part. of *exordior*, to begin), *commencement, preamble*.

expedio, 4, *free from entanglement, arrange, explain* (*ex, pes*).

exscidium, -i, n. *cutting off, destruction* (*ex, scindo*).

exsequor, -i, -secutus sum, *follow out, relate*.

exta, -orum, n. *the larger internal organs of the body*.

extundo, -ēre, -tūdi, -tusum, *to hammer out, to produce laboriously*.

exubero, 1, *abound, teem with*.

exuo, -ēre, -ui, -utum, *put off*.

falx, falcis, f. *pruning-hook*.

far, farris, n. *spelt*: also used in plur. for corn in general.

fas, indecl. n. *divine law, what religion permits*.

fascis, -is, m. *a bundle*: plur. (1) *the rods and axe carried before the highest magistrates*; (2) *high office, especially consulship*.

fatum, -i, n., (1) *a prophecy* or *prediction*; (2) *destiny* (*for*, I speak).

fauces, -ium, f. pl. *jaws* or *gullet, narrow entrance*.

favus, -i, m. *honeycomb*.

fax, facis, f. *a torch*.

fecundus, -a, -um, *fruitful*.

felix, -icis, (1) *fruit-bearing* (of trees); (2) *fortunate, happy*.

ferrugo, -inis, f. *iron grey* or *lurid colour*.

fetus, -us, m., (1) *the act of*

bringing forth, birth; (2) *off-spring, fruit.*

fetus, -a, -um, *prolific, fertile.*

fibra, -ae, f. *a fibre or filament* (of a plant or living body).

fimus, -i, m. (also **fimum**), *manure.*

fiscina, -ae, f. *a basket made of twigs or rushes.*

fissilis, -e, *easy to be split* (*findo*).

flagro, 1, *to blaze.*

flaveo -ēre, 2, *to be golden-yellow.*

flavus, *light-yellow* (as at *G.* 1, 316, of the ripe corn, while *luteus* means *deep-yellow*, as of the yoke of an egg).

follis, -is, m. *bellows.*

foris, -is, f. usually pl. *fores,* the two leaves of a door.

formido, -inis, f. *dread, horror.*

forsitan, *perhaps.*

fortunatus (perf. p. of *fortuno*, to make prosperous), *a favourite of fortune, lucky.*

foveo, -ere, fovi, fotum, *keep warm, cherish.*

fragilis, -e, *easily broken.*

fragor, -oris, m. *a crashing sound.*

frango, -ere, fregi, fractum, *break, crunch.*

fraxinus, -i, f. *ash-tree.*

frendeo or **frendo,** -ui, fresum or fressum, 2 and 3, *gnash the teeth.*

fretum, -i, n. *strait* (of the sea) (Eng. Firth).

frumentum, -i, n. *corn.* Plur. is used esp. of standing grain, 1, 150.

frux, frugis, f. usually in plur. **fruges,** -um, *fruits* of the earth in general, whereas **fructus** generally denotes *fruit of trees* and **frumen-**

tum, *grain* (from root of *fruor*).

fuco, 1, *to stain.*

fucus, -i, m., (1) *lichen used as a red dye*; (2) gum with which the bees stop crevices; (3) *a drone.*

fugio, -ēre, -i, -itum, *flee, steal* or *move silently.*

fulica, -ae, f. *a coot*; the bird is slaty-black, from *fuligo,* soot or black paint.

fulmino, 1, *hurl lightning.*

funda, -ae, f., (1) *a sling*; (2) *casting-net.*

fundamen, -inis, n. *foundation.*

fundus, -i, m. *an estate.*

furca, -ae, f. *a two-pronged fork.*

furor, -is, m. *madness* (much stronger than *insania*).

galea, -ae, f. *helmet.*

gemma, -ae, f., (1) *a bud*; (2) *a precious stone, or a vessel made from one.*

generatim, *after their kind.*

genialis, -e, *belonging to one's genius, festive.*

genitalis, -e, *birth-giving.*

germen, -inis, n. *a shoot, bud.*

gilvus, -a, -um, *pale-yellow* (German *gelb*).

glans, -dis, f. *an acorn*, used collectively at 1, 8.

glaucus, -a, -um, *greyish*, also *fierce* (Gk word, originally 'gleaming,' specially of the eyes of the warlike Athena).

globus, -i, m. *a ball.*

glomero, 1, *gather into a ball*; passive, *crowd together* (*glomus,* a ball of thread).

gluten, -inis, n. *glue.*

grandis, -e, *large, huge.*

grando, -inis, f. *hail.*

gratia, -ae, f., (1) *favour with others, friendship*; (2) *beauty*

(post-Augustan); (3) *favour
to others, kindness*; (4)
gratitude (*gratus* develops
its meaning on the same
lines).

gravidus, -a, -um, *heavy*.

gremium, -ii, n. *lap, bosom*.

grus, gruis, f. *a crane*.

gurges, -itis, m., (1) *whirlpool*;
(2) *stream* or *sea*.

hactenus, *thus far*.

haurio, -ire, -si, -stum, *to
drink, inhale*.

haustus, -us, m. *a draught*.

hedera, -ae, f. *ivy*.

herba, -ae, f. *grass, blade of
corn, an herb*.

hiems, -is, f., (1) *winter*; (2) *a
storm* (Sanskrit, *himas,
snow*).

hinnitus, -us, m. *neighing*.

hio, 1, *yawn, gape at*.

hirtus, -a, -um, *shaggy*.

holus, -eris, n. *vegetables*.

horreo, -ēre, -ui, *to be rough, to
bristle*.

horreum, -i, n. *barn*.

humerus, -i, m. *shoulder*.

humilis, -e, *on the ground,
cowering* (*humus*).

Hyades, -um, f. seven stars in
the head of Taurus (lit. ' the
Rainers').

hydrus, -i, m. *water-snake* (Gk
hudōr, water).

Hyperboreus, -a, -um, *belonging to the Hyperboreans*, a
fabulous people in the extreme North.

Iacchus, -i, m. poetic name of
Bacchus.

īdem, eadem, īdem, *the same*:
also used adverbially *at the
same time, also, nevertheless*.

ignavus, -a, -um, *slothful,
idle*.

ilex, -icis, f. *holm-oak* or *evergreen oak*.

illaudatus, -a, -um, *not praised*,
i.e. *detested*.

illudo, -ĕre, -si, -sum, *sport
with, jeer at* (see n. on 11,
464).

imago, -inis, f. *likeness, echo*
(root of *imitor*).

imber, -bris, m. *heavy rain*.

immanis, -e, (1) *monstrous in
size*; (2) *monstrous in character, savage* (*in, manus*
(old Latin) 'good.' From
same root as Sanscrit *ma*,
' to measure,' seen in *metior*;
both senses may be thus
explained).

immensus, -a, -um, *boundless*
(*in, metior*).

immitis, -e, *cruel*.

immitto, -ĕre, -isi, -issum, *send
against, let loose, ingraft*.

immundus, -a, -um, *foul* (*in,
mundus*, clean).

impendo, -ĕre, -di, -sum, *pay
out, spend*.

impius, -a, -um, *ungodly,
wanting in natural feeling*
(see *pietas*).

importunus, -a, -um (opposite
of *opportunus*), *ill-omened,
unseasonable*.

improbus, -a, -um, *not according to the standard*, (1)
monstrous, excessive; (2)
morally bad, wicked.

imprudens, -ntis, *unforeseeing,
off one's guard* (*in* and
prudens =*providens*).

inamabilis, -e, *unloveable, hateful*.

incautus, -a, -um, *heedless*.

incedo, -ĕre, -essi, -essum,
march on, befall, occur.

incipio, -ĕre, -cepi, -ceptum,
act. and neut. *begin*.

incoho, 1, v. a. and n. *begin*.

increbresco, -ĕre, -ui, *to become stronger* or *more frequent*.

increpito, 1, freq. *to keep taunting*.

increpo, -are, -ui, -itum, *to make a flapping noise*.

incudo, -ĕre, -di, -sum, *to forge, indent* (*incus*, an anvil).

Indigetes, -um, m. the deified heroes of a country (*indu* = *in*, *gigno*).

indignor, 1, *am angry*.

indignus, -a, -um, *unworthy, undeserved* or *cruel* (of punishment).

indulgentia, -ae, f. *tenderness, clemency*.

infandus, -a, -um, *unutterable, monstrous* (*in*, *fari*).

infecundus, -a, -um, *unfertile*.

inflo, 1, *blow into*.

ingemino, 1, v. a. and n. *redouble*.

ingenium, -i, n. *natural quality* (*in* and *gigno*), esp. *of gift of mind*, *genius*.

ingens, -tis, *huge* (see Conway, *Class. Review* for 1912, pp. 251 ff.).

inhio, 1, v. a. and n. *gape, open wide*.

iniquus, -a, -um, *uneven, immoderate, cruel*.

inops, -opis, *without means, poor*.

insector, 1, dep. *pursue*.

insero, -ĕre, -evi, -itum, *implant, graft*.

inspico, 1, *to make pointed* (*spica*, a spike).

instituo, -ĕre, -ui, -utum, (1) *establish*; (2) *teach*.

insulto, 1, *bound over, trample on*.

inter, prep. *between*, as adv. *here and there*, II, 366.

intubum, -i, n. *succory* or *endive*.

inumbro, 1, *overshadow*.

invigilo, 1, *to be watchful over*.

invito, 1, *invite, entertain*.

ipse, -a, -um, *spontaneously, of one's own accord*, as at II, 459.

irreparabilis, -e, *not recoverable*.

irriguus, -a, -um, (act.) *watering, irrigating* (*in* and *rigo*, to water).

irroro, 1, *to wet with dew* (*in*, *ros*).

iuba, -ae, f. *mane*.

iugum, -i, n. *yoke*.

iuvencus, -i, m. *a bullock*.

lăbor, -oris, m. *toil, hardship, distress*.

labrum, -i, n. *lip*.

lacertus, -i, m. (1) *lizard*; (2) *upper arm*.

lacrima, -ae, f. *tear, gum* (of plants).

laetus, -a, -um, *glad*, (of crops) *rich*.

laevus, -a, -um, *on the left*.

lamina, -ae, f. *a thin piece of metal, blade*.

laniger, -era, -crum, *wool-bearing*.

lappa, -ae, f. *a burr*.

laqueus, -i, m. *noose, snare*.

Lar, Laris, m. commonly pl. Lares, *household gods, home* (originally the presiding spirit of the land belonging to the household).

Larius, -i, m. (sc. *lacus*), Lago di Como.

laxus, -a, -um, *loose*.

legumen, -inis, n. anything gathered (*lego*), not cut like corn, a plant bearing pods, beans, etc.

lembus, -i, m. *skiff*.

Lenaeus, -a, -um, *belonging to the wine-press* (Gk *lenos*); epithet of Bacchus.

lentus, -a, -um, (1) *flexible, sticky*; (2) *slow*.

lex, legis, f. *a law, agreement*.

Liber, -eri, m. a name of Bacchus.

liber, -ri, m. *inner bark of a tree, book*.

libo, 1, *taste of, sip, make a libation*.

libro, 1, *to balance* (*libra*, a pair of scales).

limes, -itis, m. *a cross-path, boundary*.

limus, -i, m. *mud*.

lino, -ĕre, levi, litum, *smear*.

linter, -tris, f. *boat*.

linum, -i, n. *flax*: lina, pl. *a drag-net*.

liquidus, -a, -um, *liquid, transparent*.

lolium, -i, n. *tares*.

lumbus, -i, m. *loin*.

luo, -ere, lui, luitum, *wash, cleanse, expiate*.

lupinus, -i, m. (also **lupinum**) *lupin*.

lustro, 1, *to purify by a sacrifice and solemn procession, to traverse* (*luo*).

lustrum, -i, n. *a morass, haunt* (of wild beasts).

luxurio, 1, *abound in*.

macula, -ae, f. *spot*.

Maecenas, -atis, m. C. Cilnius Maecenas, the prime minister of Augustus, patron of Virgil and Horace; any patron of literature.

maereo, 2, v. a. and n. *mourn*.

manes, -ium, m. *the spirits of the dead* (old Latin *manus*, good. *Manes*, probably 'good spirits').

maniplus, -i, m. contr. from **manipulus**, *a handful, bundle*.

mano, 1, *flow, trickle*.

mansuesco, -ere, -suevi, -suetum, v. a. and n. *to make or to become tame or gentle* (accustom to the hand).

massa, -ae, f. *lump, block*.

maturo, 1, v. a. and n. (1) *to make or grow ripe*; (2) *to do in good time, make haste*.

Mavortius, -a, -um, *martial* (*Mavors* = Mars).

medico, 1, *to heal, sprinkle with juice of herbs*.

melisphyllum, -i, n. *balm* (Gk *honey-leaf*).

menstruus, -a, -um, *happening each month*.

merges, -itis, f. *a sheaf*.

mergus, -i, m. *gull* (*mergo*, plunge).

merops, -opis, f. *bee-eater*.

messis, -is, f. *harvest, crop*.

messor, -oris, m. *reaper*.

metallum, -i, n. *a mine, ore* (a word borrowed from Greek).

mico, -are, -ui, *move quickly to and fro, twitch*.

miseror, 1, dep. *pity*.

modo, *only*: with subj. = **dummodo**, *if only*.

molior, -iri, -itus sum, dep. *to do, make or move anything requiring great effort*.

mollis, -e, *soft, elastic*.

mox, *soon, presently*.

mugitus, -us, m. *lowing*.

munio, 4, *fortify, build*.

munus, -eris, n. *office, tribute, duty*.

murmur, -uris, n. *a humming or booming sound*.

musso, 1, *mutter*.

mustum, -i, n. *new or unfermented wine*.

myrtetum, -i, n. *myrtle-grove*.

myrtum, -i, n. *myrtle-berry*.

mysticus, -a, -um, *connected with religious rites at the Mysteries*.

nanciscor, -i, -nactus sum, dep. *obtain, find.*

narcissus, -i, m. *narcissus.*

naris, -is, f. *nostril.*

nato, 1, *to swim.*

nebula, -ae, f. *vapour lying low, mist* (contrasted with *nubes*, a cloud).

nec dum, *not yet.*

nefas, n. indecl. *what divine law forbids.*

nepos, -otis, m. *grandson.*

Neptunus, -i, m., (1) god of the sea; (2) the sea itself.

nequiquam, *in vain*, of an attempt which comes to nothing (*frustra*, of the person whose effort is disappointed).

nex, necis, f. *violent death* (*neco*).

nidus, -i, m. *nest, a nestling.*

niteo, -ēre, -ui, v. n. *to glisten, to flourish.*

nitrum, -i, n. *native soda.*

niveus, -a, -um, *snow-white.*

no, 1, *swim, float.*

noctua, -ae, f. *the small owl* (see n. on 1, 403).

nodus, -i, m. *a knot.*

novalis, -e, also used as subst. (sc. *terra*), *fallow.*

numen, -inis, n., (1) *a nod* (i.e. *a command*); (2) *a being with a will, a Divinity* (see n. on IV, 505).

obicio, -ere, -eci, -ectum, *throw in the way, place as a barrier.*

obnitor, -i, -nixus, dep. *strive against*: **obnixus**, *firm-set.*

obnoxius, -a, -um, *liable to punishment, beholden to, indebted to* (*ob* and *noxa*, a hurt or crime).

obscenus, -a, -um, *filthy, ill-boding.*

observo, 1, *take note of, pay respect to.*

obtundo, -ēre, -tŭdi, -tunsum and -tusum, *to beat against, blunt.*

obvius, -a, -um, *in the way, meeting.*

oculus, -i, m. *an eye, the bud of a plant.*

odoratus, -a, -um, *scented.*

offendo, -ēre, -di, -sum, *strike against.*

oleaster, -tri, m. *wild olive.*

Olympus, -i, m., (1) a mountain in Thrace where the Gods were believed to dwell; (2) heaven.

opaco, 1, *to overshadow.*

opacus, -a, -um, *shaded.*

operio, -ire, -ui, opertum, *to hide.*

opportunus, -a, -um, *seasonable, suitable* (Cicero defines it as 'in fitting time' and =*occasio*. It has no connexion with *portus*, a harbour).

ora, -ae, f. *edge, coast.*

orbita, -ae, f. *track of a wheel* (*orbis*).

Orcus, -i, m. the Lower World or one of its Deities.

orgia, -orum, n. pl. a wild feast of Bacchus by night.

ornus, -i, f. see n. on II, 111.

ostrum, -i, n. *the blood of the sea-snail, purple dye, cloth stained with purple.*

ovo, 1, *exult, rejoice.*

palaestra, -ae, f. *wrestling-place, bout of wrestling.*

Palatium, -i, n. one of the Seven Hills of Rome.

palea, -ae, f. *chaff.*

Pales, -is, f. a deity of sheep and cattle.

palmes, -itis, m. *a vine-shoot.*

pampinus, -i, c. *a vine-shoot.*

Pandion, -ionis, m., (1) King of Athens, changed into a

nightingale; (2) the night-ingale.

papaver, -eris, n. *a poppy.*

parcus, -a, -um, *thrifty.*

pario, -ĕre, peperi, partum, *to bring forth, acquire*: **partum** as subst. *acquisitions.*

partior -iri, -itus sum, dep. *to divide.*

parturio, 4 (desiderative v.), *desire to bring forth, bring forth.*

pastus, -us, m. *feeding, pasture.*

patrius, -a, -um, *belonging to one's father or country.*

patŭlus, -a, -um, *wide open.*

pavor, -oris, m. *panic fear.*

pecten, -inis, m. *comb, shuttle.*

pecus, -ŏris, n. *cattle*, collectively, *a herd* (from the same root as German *Vieh*, 'cattle,' whence comes our own *fee*, 'a payment.' Early coin was stamped with an ox's head).

pecus, -ŭdis, f. *a single head of cattle, a beast.*

pedica, -ae, f. *a snare.*

pelăgus, -i, n. *the open sea, the main.*

Penates, -ium, m. *household gods, home, dwelling* (originally the *di P.* meant the spirits who guard the household store of food, *penus*).

peragro, 1, *to roam over* (*per, ager*).

perfero, -ferre, -tuli, -latum, *bear to the end, endure.*

perfundo, -ĕre, -fudi, -fusum, *steep.*

perhibeo, 2, *bring forward, assert.*

periurium, -i, n. *false swearing.*

pernix, -icis, *swift.*

petulcus, -a, -um, *butting* (*peto*).

pietas, -atis, f. (dutiful conduct towards parents, the Gods and country): (1) *filial affection*; (2) *piety*; (3) *patriotism.*

Also (of feeling due from higher to lower), *pity.*

pinguis, -e, *fat, fruitful.*

pix, picis, f. *pitch.*

plango, -ĕre, -nxi, -nctum, v. a. and n. *to strike, beat* (specially of sound), *to beat the breast, wail.*

planta, -ae, f. *sprout, slip for grafting.*

platanus, -i, f. *plane-tree.*

Pleiades, -um, f. *the Seven Stars, Pleiads* (lit. 'the Sailing Stars,' as they rose at the beginning of summer; Gk *pleo*, I sail).

poculum, -i, n. *a drinking-cup, draught.*

pone, adv. and prep. *behind.*

pŏpuleus, -a, -um, *of a poplar tree* (*populus*).

portitor, -oris, m. *carrier, ferry-man.*

postis, -is, m. *a door-post.*

praecipuus, -a, -um, *special* (*prae, capio*).

praedor, -ari, -atus sum, dep. *to plunder.*

praedurus, -a, -um, *exceedingly hard.*

praeruptus, -a, -um, *broken in front, precipitous.*

praescisco, -ĕre, -scivi, -scitum, *learn beforehand* (inceptive from *scio*).

praesens, -ntis, *present, ready to help.*

praesepe, -is, n. *stables, stall, hive* (*prae, saepio*).

praetendo, -ĕre, -di, -tum, *stretch forward or in front of.*

praetexo, -ĕre, -ui, -xtum, *weave in front, fringe.*

prenso, or **prehenso**, 1, *catch at repeatedly, lay hold on* (freq. from *prehendo*).

procudo, -ĕre, -di, -sum, *beat out, sharpen.*

pronus, -a, -um, *leaning for-*

ward, bending or moving downward.

propago, -inis, f. *pegging forward*, 'layering' *plants.*

propero, 1, v. n. and a. *hasten, make in haste.*

protinus, *forthwith.*

proventus, -us, m. *produce, yield* (neither *p.* nor *provenio*, to be born, occur in Cicero).

prudens, -tis, *foreseeing, sagacious* (contracted from *providens*).

pruina, -ae, f. *hoar-frost.*

prunum, -i, n. *a plum.*

pullus, -i, m. *young animal, colt.*

purpura, -ae, f. *purple.*

purpureus, -a, -um, *purple, bright coloured.*

puteus, -i, m. *a well* (contr. with *fons*, a spring).

quadrigae, -arum, f. *four-horse chariot.*

quaero, -ēre, -sivi, -situm, *seek, enquire, obtain.*

quasso, 1, v. a. and n. *to shake.*

quernus, -a, -um, *belonging to an oak.*

quippe, *for, in fact, since.*

rabidus, -a, -um, *mad, fierce.*

racemus, -i, m. *a cluster.*

rapidus, -a, -um (with active force), *scorching, devouring* (n. on II, 321).

rapio, -ere, -ui, raptum, *snatch, sweep.*

raptim, *hurriedly.*

rapto, 1, freq. *seize, whirl away.*

rarus, -a, -um, *thin; here and there* (of things), *standing apart.*

rastrum, -i, n. (plural also **rastri**), *hoe, rake (rado).*

raucus, -a, -um, *hoarse.*

recludo, -ēre, -si, -sum, *unclose, open.*

refero, -ferre, -tuli, -latum, *carry back, re-echo.*

reformido, 1, *to dread.*

refundo, -ēre, -di, -sum, *pour back.*

religio, -ionis, f. *religious scruples* (see n. on I, 270).

relinquo, -ēre, -liqui, -lictum, *to leave, abandon.*

remigium, -i, n. *rowing, oars* (*remex*, a rower).

remitto, -ēre, -misi, -missum, *loosen, cause to yield.*

repeto, -ēre, -ivi, -itum, *to seek again, try to recover.*

repono, -ēre, -posui, -positum, *lay back, store up*; partic. *repostus* for *repositus* (see n. on III, 527).

resolvo, -ēre, -vi, -solutum, *to unloose.*

respondeo, -ēre, -i, -sum, *to answer, suit.*

resulto, 1, freq. *leap back (re, salio).*

retinaculum, -i, n. *a band.*

rigor, -oris, m. *stiffness.*

rimosus, -a, -um, *full of chinks* (*rima*).

rivus, 1, m. *small stream; lode.*

robigo, -inis, f. *rust.*

rosarium, -i, n. *rose-garden.*

rostrum, -i, n. *beak (rodo).*

rubeo, 2, v. n. *am red.*

rubeus, -a, -um, *made from the bramble* (*rubus*).

rubicundus, -a, -um, *ruddy.*

rutilus, -a, -um, *gleaming.*

saburra, -ae, f. *ballast* (*sabulo*, coarse sand).

saeculum, -i, n. *a generation* of the human race.

saepes, -is, f. *hedge, fence.*

saepta, -orum, n. pl. *enclosures.*

saevio, 4, *to rage.*

salix, -icis, f. *a willow.*

saltem, *at least.*

saltus, -us, m., (1) *forest-pasture*; (2) *woodland*; (3) *a ravine*.

sanctus, -a, -um, *inviolable, reverenced, pure* (*sacer* used of things belonging to the gods, like a temple; *sanctus,* of what is akin to the character of the gods, holy, held in reverence).

sapor, saporis, m. the *flavour inherent* in anything.

satio, -onis, f. *sowing, planting.*

saturo, 1, *to fill full, saturate.*

saxosus, -a, -um, *rocky.*

saxum, -i, n. *a large stone, rock, boulder* (*lapis* = stone as material, or small in mass).

scaber, -bra, -brum, *rough.*

scilicet, *doubtless, in fact.*

scrobis, -is, f. *ditch.*

securus, -a, -um, *free from care* (*se* = *sine, cura*).

sedes, -is, f. *home.*

seges, -etis, f., (1) *a cornfield*; (2) *the crop in the field.*

segnis, -e, *slothful.*

semen, -inis, n. *seed, a young plant.*

serenus, -a, -um, *bright, clear.*

Seres, -um, m. Orientals, probably Chinese.

serpyllum, -i, n. *wild thyme* (*serpo,* from its spreading habit).

serra, -ae, f. *a saw.*

serus, -a, -um, *late* (Fr. *soir*).

servo, 1, *perceive, watch.*

sidus, -eris, n. a constellation or any large heavenly body (esp. as marking the seasons: *stella* = any star).

signo, 1, *mark out, stain.*

signum, -i, n. *sign, token.*

siliqua, -ae, f. *pod.*

silva, -ae, f., (1) *wood*; (2) *stalks of plants.*

silvestris, -e, *belonging to the woods, wild.*

simplex, -icis, *simple, uniform.*

simulacrum, -i, n. *image, phantom.*

sinus, -us, m. *a bent surface, a hollow, bosom, orifice.*

situs, -us, m., (1) *situation*; (2) *that which is left alone* (*sino*), *mildew, scurf* (on surface of untilled land).

sollicito, 1, *to stir up, disturb* (*sollus,* whole, and *cieo*).

solum, -i, n. *ground.*

sopor, -oris, m. *deep sleep.*

spadix, -icis, c., a palm-branch with its dates. As adj. the colour of dates, *chestnut.*

spatium, -i, n. *space.* Plural, the laps of the race-course or the passing over these of racers.

species, -ei, f., (1) *outward aspect, shape*; (2) *semblance*; (3) *kind.*

spectaculum, -i, n. *a show.*

specto, 1, *gaze at, examine.*

speculor, 1, dep. *spy out, look out for.*

spelunca, -ae, f. *cave.*

spiculum, -i, n. *dart, sting* (*spica,* anything pointed).

spinus, -i, f. *the sloe-tree* or *blackthorn.*

spira, -ae, f. *a coil, spire.*

spiramentum, -i, n. *breathing-place, crevice.*

spiro, (1) *breathe, emit fragrance*; (2) *heave.*

spuma, -ae, f. *foam, froth.*

squaleo, -ere, -ui, *to be rough* or *neglected*: **squalens,** *scaly.*

squama, -ae, f. *a scale.*

stabulum, -i, n. *stall.*

stagnum, -i, n. *standing water, pool* (*sto*).

statio, -onis, f. *a fixed abode* (*sto*).

sterno, -ĕre, stravi, stratum, *to lay low.*

stipo, 1, *pack tight*.

stipula, -ae, f. *stubble*.

stirps, -is, f. *the stock* or *root* of a tree.

strepito, 1, freq. *make a noise, caw* (*strepo*).

stridor, -oris, m. *any harsh sound* (*strideo*).

stringo, -ĕre, -inxi, -ictum, (1) *bind tight*; (2) *strip off*.

studium, -i, n. *interest, zeal*; pl. *pursuits*.

stuppeus, -a, -um, *made of tow*.

subeo, -ire, -ii, -ītum, *come up from beneath*.

subigo, -ĕre, -egi, -actum, (1) *conquer*; (2) *dig up thoroughly* (a term of husbandry); (3) *drive up*.

sublabor, -i, -lapsus sum, dep. *slip under, sink*.

sublimis, -e, *aloft*.

submitto, 3, *to rear up*.

suboles, -is, f. *shoot* (of a tree), *progeny, race* (*sub* and *ol*, to grow, as in *ad-ol-esco*).

succedo, -ĕre, -essi, -essum, *to go from below, mount up*.

sudo, 1, *to sweat*.

sudus, -a, -um, *dry, cloudless* (*se* = *sine, udus*, moist).

sulcus, -i, m. *furrow*.

supero, 1, v. a. and n. *to conquer, to be in abundance*.

suscito, 1, *arouse, stir up*.

suspicio, -ĕre, -xi, -ctum, *to look up at*.

sustineo, -ēre, -ui, -tentum, *to support*.

tabularium, -i, n. *archives*.

tarde, *slowly*.

taxus, -i, f. *yew-tree*.

tellus, -uris, f. *the earth* (almost solely in poetry), also personified.

tempero, 1, *regulate*; **temperare sibi**, *to restrain one's self*.

tempestas, -atis, f., (1) *a portion of time*; *a season*; (2) *weather* (good or bad); (3) *a storm*.

tempto, 1, *handle, attempt*.

tener, -era, -erum, m., (1) *tender*; (2) *young*.

tenor, -oris, m. *course, mode of existence*.

tepidus, -a, -um, *lukewarm*.

tero, -ĕre, trivi, tritum, *rub, wear*.

terra, -ae, f., (1) *earth, soil*; (2) *a country, territory*; **terrae**, pl. *the world*.

testudo, -inis, f. *tortoise, tortoise-shell*.

thalamus, -i, m. *chamber* (Gk).

thymbra, -ae, f. *savory* (the plant).

tilia, -ae, f. *lime-tree*.

tinguo, -ĕre, -xi, -nctum, *wet, dip*.

tondeo, -ēre, totondi, tonsum, *shear, lop*.

torpeo, -ēre, -ui, *to be sluggish*.

torus, -i, m. *anything which bulges, like muscles in the arm*; *muscle, a cushion*.

tractus, -us, m., (1) *a dragging*; (2) *course, track*.

trahea, -ae, f. *a threshing-board*.

trapetum, -i, n. *an oil press*.

trepido, 1, *to hurry in alarm, be in agitation*.

trepidus, -a, -um, *trembling, simmering, agitated*.

tribolus, -i, m., (1) an instrument with three prongs resting on the earth and one standing up, used for impeding cavalry; (2) a thistle resembling it.

tribulum, -i, n. *a wooden sledge for threshing*, studded below with sharp teeth of iron or flint: hence the late-Latin word *tribulatio*, 'tribulation.'

tristis, -e, (1) *sad*; (2) *bitter*.

tropaeum, -i, n. *a trophy* (Gk *trope*, a turning, set up when the enemy turned back).

trudo, -ĕre, -si, -sum, *thrust*.

truncus, -i, m. *bole* or *trunk* of a tree: 'a truncheon' in grafting.

tumesco, -ĕre, -ui, *to grow swelled*.

tumultus, -i, m. *tumult, a rising in arms* within Italy, *civil war*.

tunica, -ae, f. *under-garment, sheath*.

turbidus, -a, -um, *muddy*.

turbo, -inis, m. *whirlwind*.

tureus, -a, -um, *of frankincense*.

turifer, -a, -um, *incense-bearing* (*tus, turis, fero*).

turpis, -e, *foul, ugly*.

udus, -a, -um, *moist*.

ulmus, -i, f. *elm-tree*.

ululo, 1, *howl*.

umecto, 1, *to moisten* (*umor* (*humor*), moisture).

ungula, -ae, f. *hoof* (*unguis*).

urgeo, -ēre, ursi, (1) *press, push*; (2) *press hard, beset* (in war); (3) *oppress, crush*.

uva, -ae, f. *a bunch of grapes*.

vallus, -i, m. *a stake*.

vannus, -i, m. *winnowing-fan*.

varius, -a, -um, *manifold* (diversus, *differing* or *opposite*).

velum, -i, n. *sail*.

vena, -ae, f. *vein*.

venenum, -i, n. *poison, dye*.

vepres, -is, m. *thorn-bush*.

verbena, -ae, f. usu. plur. plants or tree-branches used in religious acts.

verber, -eris, n. *lash, thong* (of sling, etc.).

verbero, 1, *to lash*.

versus, -us, m. *furrow, row, line* (of verse).

vertex, -icis, m., (1) *a whirl of water or wind*; (2) *the top of the human head or summit of a mountain* (*verto*).

verutus, -a, -um, *armed with darts* (*veru*).

vescus, -a, -um, *small*.

vestigium, -i, n. *a footstep*.

veternus, -i, m. *lethargy, drowsiness*.

vetus, -eris, adj. *old* (see antiquus).

vicia, -ae, f. *vetch*.

victus, -us, m. *means of living, food*.

viduo, 1, *to widow, bereave*.

vilis, -e, *cheap*.

vimen, -inis, n. *osier*.

vindemia, -ae, f. *vintage*.

vinetum, -i, n. *plantation of vines*.

violarium, -i, n. *violet-bed*.

vireo, -ēre, no perf. or sup. *to be green*.

virgeus, -a, -um, *made of twigs* (*virga*).

virgultum, -i, n. *a thicket*.

virus, -i, n. *poison*.

viscum, -i, n., (1) *mistletoe berry*; (2) *bird-lime made from it*.

vitis, -is, f. *a vine*.

Volcanus, -i, m. *Vulcan*, the Fire-god, *fire*.

volito, 1, freq. *keep flying*.

vomo, -ĕre, -ui, -itum, *disgorge*.

votum, -i, n. (1) *solemn vow*; (2) *prayer*.

vulgo, 1, *make common*.

Zephyrus, -i, m. *West wind*.

GENERAL INDEX TO NOTES